MasterChef
STREET
FOOD
- OF THE WORLD -

MasterChef
STREET
FOOD
- OF THE WORLD -

Genevieve Taylor
with contributions from
MasterChef Champions
Photography by David Loftus

Absolute Press

An imprint of Bloomsbury Publishing Plc
50 Bedford Square, London, WC1B 3DP, UK
29 Earlsfort Terrace, Dublin 2, Ireland

www.bloomsbury.com
ABSOLUTE PRESS and the A. logo are trademarks of Bloomsbury Publishing Plc

First published 2017

British Library Cataloguing-in-Publication Data
A catalogue record for this book is available from the British Library.
Library of Congress Cataloguing-in-Publication data has been applied for.

ISBN: HB: 9781472909169
ePDF: 9781472946201
ePub: 9781472946218

4 6 8 10 12 11 9 7 5

Printed and bound in China by C&C Offset Printing Co., Ltd.

Bloomsbury Publishing Plc makes every effort to ensure that the papers used in the manufacture
of our books are natural, recyclable products made from wood grown in well-managed forests.
Our manufacturing processes conform to the environmental regulations of the country of origin.
To find out more about our authors and books visit www.bloomsbury.com. Here you will find extracts,
author interviews, details of forthcoming events and the option to sign up for our newsletters.

CONTENTS

INTRODUCTION

Welcome to the amazing world of MasterChef street food!

The proliferation of street food is perhaps *the* foodie phenomenon of the past decade and one that's been pretty much impossible to miss. Culinary entrepreneurs across the globe are bringing towns and cities alive with hip food trucks, buzzing night markets and thronging food festivals. It seems we just cannot get enough of this carefree, sociable way of eating and its popularity continues to rise and rise.

Yet street food is far from a recent fad. There is evidence of Aztec markets having had vendors selling snacks to hungry shoppers, including the still very much beloved guacamole! In ancient Rome food was normally bought and eaten on the street by the urban poor who didn't have kitchens of their own to cook in, whilst in medieval London, fresh oysters, pies and baked apples were all commonly eaten on the roadsides.

In these pages myself and 13 MasterChef champions from around the globe bring you a collection of mouthwatering recipes spanning a kaleidoscope of colours, flavours, textures and sheer taste sensations.

So why bother to make street food at home when there's so much good stuff out there on the real streets? For me and our MasterChef contributors it's about bringing a bit of adventurous spirit into your kitchen and transporting you to another place, perhaps stretching yourself from a cooking point of view into unknown territory. If you love food then surely one of the most tantalising parts of travelling is to immerse yourself in the edible delights and eating on the street can connect you to a culture in a way dining in a fancy restaurant never will. And whilst you might not have the time, money or inclination to go roaming the world for tasty things to eat, you can really easily bring a sense of adventure and wanderlust into your home kitchen.

With a lifelong passion for travel, some of the most memorable meals of my life have been eaten on the go. My mind was blown by a fragrant Malaysian curry eaten at a bustling night market in Borneo and a steaming hot dog from a sidewalk cart in New York, slathered in vivid yellow mustard, was perhaps the best I'd ever eaten. I will never forget the ginger-heavy seafood stir fry at the crab market in Kampot in Cambodia, devoured greedily whilst watching the fishermen haul their catch onto land, or for the incredibly simple but impossible to beat – fresh pomegranate seeds tapped from the shell into my cupped palms by an elderly woman on a Cretan roadside – these are just a fraction of the things lodged deep in my mind.

This book is divided loosely by the continents of the world, and within these vibrant pages you will find the very best examples from the streets of the Americas, Europe, Africa and the Middle East, India and Asia. Some recipes will be instantly familiar – such as Marc Boissieux's banoffee crepes, Dhruv Baker's *pakoras* or Claudia Sandoval's fish taco – and who could write on this subject and not include the globally ubiquitous beef burger, the classic British fish and chips or the world famous pad Thai? But there is plenty within that will surprise and delight: try Tim Anderson's *daigaku imo*, a delicious take on sweet potatoes; or the *midye dolma*, spicy rice stuffed mussels from Turkey; or *doro wat*, an exquisitely fragrant chicken and egg stew from Ethiopia; or *mirchi bhaji*, the Indian snack of crisp battered chillies stuffed with paneer cheese. Some of the recipes in this book will offer unique and unexpected twists on well-known favourites (see Brent Owen's take on a steak and onion pie), but all recipes are recipes packed full of authentic flavour, such as Ping Coombes' *chai tau kueh*, Andy Allen's fried school of prawns, Adam Liaw's triple-fried karaage chicken rolls or Woo Wai Leong's oyster omelette to name just a few.

Think of a street food experience and it's perhaps the cuisine of hot climates that spring to mind first – the intense tropical flavours of Jamaican jerk chicken, the fragrant spices of Christine Ha's traditional spicy lemongrass beef noodle soup or the cooling delights of Indian mango and cardamon kulfi lollies. However colder parts of the world have also embraced this way of eating, with the food designed to comfort rather than invigorate, so don't just save this book for cooking during the summer months. MasterChef champions offer recipes such as Simon Wood's black pudding Scotch eggs, or *biksemad*, Anders Halskov-Jensen's traditional Danish dish made of leftovers but brilliantly served with a fried egg, or delicious *gnocco fritto*, a fried bread sandwich from Luca Manfè. There's the famous *zapiekanki* of Poland, a moreish combination of oozing cheese and garlicky mushrooms on a simple French bread pizza; or *korvapusti*, the warm cinnamon and cardamom buns of Finland; or *leberkase*, the hearty meatloaf burger of Germany, served with crunchy pickles and fiery mustard; or the utterly simple but awesomely good slow grilled short ribs from Argentina, which are perfect for a summer barbecue, but taste just as fabulous on a cold day alongside a generous glass of hearty red (Argentinian, of course!). There is plenty of year-round inspiration to be found within these pages.

Many of the recipes are straightforward and can be knocked up with ease, but others are quite involved and might stretch the cook a little. This is a MasterChef book after all, so you expect that, right? However, whether the recipes are simple or challenging, what characterises them all is a laid back approach to their eating. Street food is not food that stands on ceremony, its chilled, casual and low key, eaten messily with hands or scooped from big bowls. This is food that celebrates the very best things in life, family and friends, eating, drinking, laughter and sharing.

Let your culinary global adventure begin – happy cooking!

Genevieve Taylor

THE AMERICAS

Think of classic American street food, and no doubt the first thing that springs to mind is a delicious fully loaded burger or a steaming hotdog, dripping with sweet onions and zingy mustard, but once you include central and south America into the mix the food is as colourful and varied as anywhere on the globe. With recipes stretching from Canada to Argentina and pretty much everywhere in between, this is a continent that embraces street eats with both hands.

The state of Louisiana excels at tasty things stuffed between bread, and hole-in-the-wall sandwich shops are wildly popular. Try the brilliantly named muffeleta, an Italian inspired layered cheese and meat supremo, or the legendary braised beef po' boy, a full fat, dripping down your chin extravaganza! Head down into central and South America and ground corn often replaces wheat as the carb of choice. Try the comforting steamed cornbread tamales, or my favourite, white maize arepas – think of them as sturdy, slightly chewy pitta pockets into which you can stuff all manner of delicious fillings. Claudia Sandoval offers a great take on a Mexican fish taco – definitely one to try. While in the Caribbean, the Indian influence is easy to spot, such as the chickpea curry in the trini doubles or the exquisite spicing on jerk chicken.

America has always been an epicentre for immigration, and this is mirrored in the street food, with cultural influences from far and wide. Simply put, in this diverse continent you can get whatever kind of food you want, whenever you want to eat it.

Not just limited to the USA, mac 'n' cheese is a truly global comfort food, more recently adopted on the street as a beloved staple of food trucks and festivals alike. This is one of those recipes that can be twisted and turned almost infinitely to suit your own taste; this just happens to be my version as it's a variant of what I grew up on.

MAC 'N' CHEESE

SERVES 4

350g short macaroni
8 rashers smoked streaky bacon (optional)
60g butter
60g plain flour
800ml milk (I used semi-skimmed, but any will do)
a dash of Worcestershire sauce
1 teaspoon English mustard
350g extra-mature Cheddar cheese, grated
freshly ground black pepper

Bring a large pan of lightly salted water to the boil and tip in the macaroni, stirring well to ensure it doesn't clump up. Boil until just tender but with plenty of bite, then drain and set aside.

Meanwhile, grill the bacon until crisp, if using. Chop it into snippets and set aside.

Melt the butter in a large saucepan set over a medium heat, then pour in the flour and stir thoroughly over the heat for a minute until you form a smooth roux. Reduce the heat to low and gradually add the milk, whisking constantly until you have dispersed the roux through the milk. Turn the heat back up to medium and bring to a steady simmer, stirring all the time, until thickened, about 3–4 minutes. Taste a little on the end of a teaspoon – it shouldn't taste floury at all; if it does, cook for another minute or so. Turn off the heat and stir through the Worcestershire sauce and mustard, and a generous grind of black pepper. Sprinkle in about three-quarters of the cheese, stirring until it has melted, then add the cooked macaroni and bacon snippets and stir to combine.

Preheat the oven to 200°C/180°C Fan/Gas Mark 6. Spoon the macaroni into a baking dish and sprinkle over the remaining cheese. Bake in the hot oven for 15–20 minutes, until the top is golden and bubbling. Serve immediately.

VARIATIONS
Feel free to put your own twist on your mac 'n' cheese using the following ideas for inspiration. Purists may complain, but this is your dinner so add whatever takes your fancy.

- Cubed mozzarella sprinkled on top adds a lovely stringy stretch once baked; grated Parmesan adds extra punch, or try smoked Cheddar or Stilton – whatever's your favourite.
- A handful of fresh breadcrumbs sprinkled over the cheese topping adds extra crunch.
- A few tomato slices under the cheese topping add extra colour (and a few vitamins!).
- Replace the bacon with crisp-fried chorizo or chopped cooked sausage, or a little leftover pulled pork or baked ham.
- Add a handful of cooked veggies, such as peas, broccoli or cauliflower.
- Give it an Italian twist with a dollop of pesto, or a handful of torn basil and a few chopped sundried tomatoes.

In years past, shrimp were a really inexpensive ingredient in Louisiana, and so became traditional in the legendary 'poor boy' sandwiches. Much more of a treat today, these crisp and spicy fried prawns make for a pretty luxurious snack.

CAJUN SHRIMP PO' BOY

MAKES 4 GENEROUS SANDWICHES

4 tablespoons mayonnaise
1 tablespoon chopped flat-leaf parsley
2 large gherkins, finely chopped
100g plain flour
1 egg
100ml milk
300g large raw peeled prawns (about 20)
a large baguette, cut into 4 lengths
a couple of handfuls of shredded crisp lettuce
2 large tomatoes, sliced

for the Cajun seasoning
2 tablespoons paprika
1 tablespoon dried oregano
1 tablespoon freshly ground black pepper
1 tablespoon garlic powder
1 tablespoon onion powder
2 teaspoons dried thyme
1–2 teaspoons chilli powder, to taste
1 teaspoon sea salt

For the Cajun seasoning, place all the ingredients in a large bowl and mix together thoroughly.

In a separate bowl, stir together the mayonnaise, parsley and gherkins. Stir through 2 teaspoons of Cajun seasoning, or to taste, and set aside.

Stir the flour through the remaining Cajun seasoning.

In another bowl, beat together the egg and milk. Line up the prawns, the flour/spice mix, egg and milk mix, and a large clean plate on the worktop. Take a prawn and dip it into the flour to coat all over, then dip into the egg and milk, then back into the flour for a second coating, before setting aside on the plate. Repeat until all the prawns have a double coating of spicy flour.

Heat the oil in a deep fat fryer to 180°C/350°F and fry the prawns in batches for about 3 minutes until golden and crisp. Drain briefly on kitchen paper.

To serve, slice the baguettes through, but leave top and bottom hinged together. If you like you can warm them briefly in a hot oven. Spread a little mayonnaise dressing inside each piece of bread and add some lettuce and tomato slices. Top with the crisp prawns and a further dollop of dressing and tuck in while hot.

Beef braised with garlic and red wine to the point of tender collapse, then stuffed into a fresh hunk of bread ... yes please! This, to my mind, is the king of the po' boys, the traditional Louisiana sub sandwiches. The debris gravy is made from all the lovely juices and caramelised bits left over from braising, thickened into a tasty sauce that soaks the bread with deliciousness. Be warned – you'll need plenty of napkins as po' boys are gorgeously messy!

Note: you will need to begin this recipe at least 8 hours before you want to eat, as the beef requires a long, slow cooking time.

SLOW-BRAISED BEEF PO' BOY WITH DEBRIS GRAVY

SERVES 6–8

1.4kg beef brisket
4 garlic cloves, sliced
2 tablespoons vegetable oil
1 large onion, finely diced
2 carrots, finely diced
500ml beef stock
250ml red wine
2–3 thyme sprigs
1 tablespoon cornflour
salt and freshly ground black
    pepper

to serve
2 large baguettes, each cut into
    3–4 pieces
Little Gem lettuce, separated
    into leaves
3 large tomatoes, sliced
3–4 gherkins, sliced lengthways
2–3 tablespoons mayonnaise

Preheat the oven to 140°C/120°C Fan/Gas Mark 1. Take a small, sharp knife and pierce deep slits all over the beef. Poke the garlic slices well into the slits, ensuring they are completely hidden within the meat so they won't fall out and burn when you are browning the beef. Season generously all over with salt and pepper.

Add half the oil to a deep flameproof casserole dish – a heavy cast-iron dish is ideal – and set over a high heat. When the oil is smoking hot, add the beef and brown well all over – the deep caramelisation adds much in terms of flavour, so do get a bit of colour into it.

Remove to a plate, reduce the heat to low and add the remaining oil to the casserole dish, followed by the onion and carrot, stirring to soften a little for a couple of minutes. Return the beef to the pan along with any juices, then pour in the beef stock and red wine and tuck in the thyme. Bring to a simmer then cover with a tight-fitting lid and slide into the oven. Allow to cook very slowly for around 6–8 hours, turning the joint every couple of hours if you can to ensure even cooking, until it is really tender. You can test whether it's ready by trying to tease the meat apart with a fork – it should give easily; if not, cook for a little longer.

Turn off the oven. Lift the meat from the casserole dish and set aside on a plate in the oven to keep warm. Place 2 tablespoons of the cooking sauce into a heatproof glass and set aside to cool. Set the casserole dish on the hob over a high heat and boil for about 10 minutes until the sauce is reduced by half. Stir the cornflour into the cooled reserved juices until you have a smooth paste. Pour into the dish and stir until the sauce thickens. Turn off the heat.

Remove the beef from the oven and cut into thick slices, dropping them into the gravy as you go and stirring to coat.

To serve, slice each piece of bread through the middle and open out, but leave top and bottom hinged together. Add a few slices of beef to each, plus a little sauce. Top with lettuce, tomato and gherkin slices and finish with a little mayonnaise. Serve immediately.

Could any dish be more 'street' than the ubiquitous burger? It's famous across the world, thanks in part to global fast-food chains, but I think the very best burgers are the ones you build yourselves, adding all the extras you fancy and leaving behind those you don't. This one is my favourite – a smoked bacon cheeseburger slathered with smoky hot mayonnaise.

Note: you will need to begin this recipe the day before you want to eat, as the brioche dough is proved overnight. The burgers can also be made the day before, as they develop a great flavour in the fridge overnight.

THE ULTIMATE BACON CHEESEBURGER

MAKES 6 FULL-SIZED BURGERS OR 12 SMALLER 'SLIDERS'

1 onion, very finely chopped or grated
2 teaspoons Marmite or other yeast extract
1 teaspoon dried mixed herbs
1kg good-quality minced beef
6 tablespoons mayonnaise
2–3 tablespoons Sriracha sauce, or to taste
smoked paprika, to taste
18 slices smoked streaky bacon
6 slices extra-mature Cheddar cheese
a handful of shredded crisp lettuce
salt and freshly ground black pepper
ketchup, to serve (optional)

for the brioche rolls
550g strong white bread flour
2 teaspoons fast-action yeast
2 teaspoons caster sugar
1 teaspoon fine salt
250ml warm milk
100g butter, softened
3 eggs, plus 1 beaten egg for glazing
vegetable oil, for greasing
2 tablespoons sesame seeds

For the brioche rolls, place the flour, yeast, caster sugar and salt in the bowl of a food mixer fitted with the paddle attachment and mix briefly until combined. Pour in the milk and add the butter and eggs. Mix slowly at first, until well combined, then increase the speed and continue to beat for a further 10 minutes. During this time the dough should become smooth, shiny and stretchy. I would not advise making this dough by hand, as it is a wet and sticky dough and much easier to make using a food mixer. Scrape the dough into a clean, lightly oiled bowl and cover with cling film. Leave to prove at room temperature for an hour, then transfer to the fridge and leave overnight.

In a large bowl, combine the onion, Marmite, herbs and salt and pepper to taste, to make a paste. Add the minced beef and mix through lightly, trying to avoid overworking the beef. Divide the mixture into 6 even-sized balls and flatten each one between the palms of your hands until about 1.5cm thick and 12cm in diameter. At this point, you can interleave the burgers with cling film or baking parchment and refrigerate until you are ready to cook.

Once the brioche has had its overnight prove, remove from the fridge and tip on to a lightly oiled worktop, kneading briefly to knock it back. Cut into 6 pieces, weighing each for accuracy if you want to ensure even-sized buns. Take each piece and roll into a ball, then flatten slightly to a thick disc. Pinch up the sides by pressing and pleating on top, working all the way round, then flip over so it's seam side down, cupping under your palm and rolling into a perfectly smooth, round bun. Repeat with the remaining pieces, placing them well spaced out on a lightly greased baking tray as you go. Leave to prove for another hour at room temperature.

For the smoky hot mayonnaise, combine the mayonnaise, Sriracha sauce and paprika in a bowl, and season to taste with black pepper. Set aside in the fridge until needed.

Preheat the oven to 200°C/180°C Fan/Gas Mark 6. Place a dish of water in the base of the oven to create a steamy atmosphere. Brush the tops of the buns with a little beaten egg and sprinkle with sesame seeds. Bake the buns for about 25–30 minutes, until a deep golden brown. Leave to cool on a wire rack.

When you are ready to eat, grill the burgers on a medium-hot barbecue or under a grill for about 3–4 minutes on each side, or until cooked to your liking. Adopt a strict one-turn-only policy with your burgers – this not only allows a caramelised crust to develop, which adds much in the flavour department, but also minimises the chance of the burgers falling apart.

Once the burgers have been turned, grill the slices of bacon until crisp. With about a minute or two to go on the burgers, top each with a slice of cheese so it begins to melt a little. Split the buns open and toast the cut sides for a minute or so.

To assemble, dollop a little smoky mayo on the base of each bun. Add some lettuce to each and top with the burger and cheese. Finally, add 3 pieces of bacon, a squeeze of ketchup, if using, or a little more mayo, and top with the other half of the bun. Serve immediately.

The gloriously named muffeleta is another top-drawer sandwich from Louisiana, this time with Italian origins. Stuffed to the gunnels with a mixture of cured meats and cheese, and layered with a punchy olive salad, this just gets better with time, and is a great street food snack.

Note: you will need to begin this recipe about 4–5 hours before you want to eat, to allow time for the focaccia to prove and the sandwich flavours to mingle.

MUFFELETA

SERVES 6–8

for the focaccia
400g strong white bread flour
1 teaspoon fast-action yeast
a pinch of fine salt
225ml hand-hot water
2 tablespoons olive oil, plus extra
    for greasing and drizzling
sea salt flakes, for sprinkling

for the olive salad
250g mixed pitted olives,
    chopped
100g roasted red peppers,
    chopped
50g sundried tomatoes, finely
    chopped
1 banana shallot, finely chopped
1 garlic clove, crushed
4 tablespoons olive oil
2 tablespoons wine vinegar (red
    or white)
1 red chilli, finely chopped
2 tablespoons chopped flat-leaf
    parsley
1 teaspoon chopped fresh
    oregano, or ½ teaspoon dried
freshly ground black pepper

for the filling
250g provolone, thinly sliced
75g coppa, thinly sliced
50g salami finocchiona (salami
    with fennel), thinly sliced
250g scamorza, thinly sliced
50g salami ventricina piccante
    (hot spiced salami), thinly
    sliced
75g mortadella, thinly sliced

For the focaccia, place the flour, yeast and a pinch of fine salt in the bowl of a food mixer with the dough hook attached. With the motor running slowly, pour in the water followed by the olive oil. Knead together for 5 minutes until soft, smooth and elastic. You can also make the dough by hand if you prefer: the kneading will take around 10 minutes. Place the dough in a lightly oiled bowl and cover with cling film. Set aside to prove for an hour or two until doubled in size.

Lightly oil a large baking tray and tip the dough on to it, pressing it out with your hands until it's around 24cm square and a generous 1cm thick. Leave to prove, uncovered and at room temperature, for a further 30 minutes.

Preheat the oven to 200°C/180°C Fan/Gas Mark 6. Poke deep finger holes all over the dough and pour over a generous drizzle of olive oil. Finish with a sprinkle of sea salt, then bake for 20–25 minutes, until golden. If you lift the loaf it should sound hollow when tapped underneath. Leave to cool on a wire rack then carefully slice through the middle, creating 2 thin squares.

Make the olive salad by mixing all the ingredients in a bowl, and season to taste with black pepper; it shouldn't need any salt because of the olives. Divide the salad between the two halves of bread, spreading it all the way to the edges. On one side of the bread, start layering up the fillings, again making sure to take them up to the edges. I start with a layer of provolone, then coppa and salami finocchiona, followed by the scamorza, salami ventricina piccante and finally the mortadella. Place the other piece of bread on top, pressing down firmly. Wrap the whole stuffed loaf tightly in cling film and set aside at room temperature for a couple of hours for the flavours to mingle. To serve, unwrap and cut into neat squares.

Brought to New Orleans by the French in the eighteenth century, beignets are crisp little doughnuts made from a rich yeasted dough. Served hot and rolled in cinnamon sugar, these make a very moreish treat. Best of all, they freeze brilliantly, so you can pop them in the fryer and enjoy them anytime you fancy.

Note: you will need to begin this recipe about 3–4 hours before you want to eat, or even the day before, to allow the dough time to prove.

BEIGNETS WITH CINNAMON SUGAR

MAKES ABOUT 28 BEIGNETS

350ml warm water
170ml evaporated milk
2 eggs
50g butter, softened
900g plain flour
100g caster sugar
1 teaspoon fast-action yeast
a pinch of salt
vegetable oil, for greasing
100g icing sugar
1 teaspoon ground cinnamon,
   or to taste

Place the water, evaporated milk, eggs and butter in the bowl of a food mixer and beat gently with the paddle attachment until combined. Add the flour, sugar, yeast and salt and continue to beat gently until well mixed in. Increase the speed and beat for another 3–4 minutes until you get a smooth, sticky dough. I would not advise making this dough by hand, as it is a wet and sticky dough and much easier made using a food mixer.

Lightly oil a large bowl and scrape the dough into it, turning it once or twice so it has a thin coating of oil all over. Cover the bowl with cling film (the oiled surface will prevent it from sticking should it rise that high) and set aside to prove for 3–4 hours on the worktop; it should double in size. You could also prove the dough in the fridge overnight.

Sift the icing sugar into a bowl and stir through the cinnamon. Set aside.

Turn out the ball of dough on to a lightly oiled worktop and slice into quarters. Roll each piece into a sausage shape of about 3cm diameter and cut on the diagonal into 2–3cm slices – you should get about 7 beignets from each quarter. If you wish to freeze a batch, space them out on a baking tray to freeze initially, then pack into a bag or tub and leave in the freezer until you want to eat (they cook from frozen so no need to defrost).

Heat the oil in a deep fat fryer to 180°C/350°F. Add about 4 or 5 beignets at a time and fry for 4 minutes until deep golden brown, carefully turning halfway with a fork to cook the other side. If cooking from frozen, add an extra minute or two to the cooking time. Drain for a few moments on kitchen paper before tossing in the cinnamon-flavoured icing sugar and setting aside on a plate. Repeat with the remaining beignets. Serve immediately while still hot.

These utterly delicious sweet tarts are said to be one of Canada's only indigenous recipes and are baked on the street and in homes across the land, with several festivals and 'food trails' dedicated to celebrating them. They are traditionally made with corn syrup to keep the texture soft and oozing; however this can be hard to find in the UK, so I've used maple syrup, as it seemed fitting, but do use corn syrup if you can find it, or even golden syrup will work.

BUTTER TARTS

MAKES 12 TARTS, SERVING ABOUT 6–8 (ONE IS NEVER QUITE ENOUGH!)

100g raisins
180g soft brown sugar
180g butter, softened
3 eggs
100ml maple syrup, or corn syrup/golden syrup
2 teaspoons vanilla extract
a large pinch of salt

for the pastry
200g plain flour, plus extra for dusting
110g cold butter, cut into 1cm cubes
4–5 tablespoons ice-cold water

you will need
a 12-hole muffin tin and a 12cm cutter (i you don't have a big enough cutter, flatten out a paper muffin case and use it as a template to cut around)

For the pastry, place the flour and butter in a food processor and pulse until you have coarse crumbs. Trickle in the water, pulsing as you go, until the mixture comes together into loose clumps. Don't overmix as you will end up with tough rather than crumbly pastry. You can also make the pastry by hand: rub the flour and butter together between your fingers and thumbs until it resembles breadcrumbs, then add the water and stir through with a knife to incorporate it, bringing the mixture together with your hands. Place the pastry on a sheet of cling film and draw up the edges, gently pressing it into a ball. Chill in the fridge for an hour.

Once the pastry has chilled, roll it out on a lightly floured worktop until it's about 2–3mm thick – the thinner the better, so each bite is all about the filling. Using a 12cm cutter, cut out 12 circles. You may need to re-roll the pastry trimmings to get all 12 circles, but if you roll it thin enough there should be plenty.

Press and fold each circle gently into place in a 12-hole muffin tin; little folds and crimps are traditional here, so don't worry about making the tarts look too perfect and neat. Chill the tin in the fridge for 30 minutes to relax the pastry and reduce shrinkage on baking.

While the pastry is chilling for the second time, make the filling. Place the raisins in a small bowl and pour over boiling water to cover. Leave to soak for 30 minutes before draining well.

Meanwhile, add the brown sugar and butter to the bowl of a food mixer and beat until smooth and creamy. You can also do this by hand with a wooden spoon and a bit of elbow grease. Add the eggs, one at a time, beating well between each addition. Then add the syrup, vanilla and salt and beat until smooth.

Preheat the oven to 220°C/200°C Fan/Gas Mark 7. Divide the drained raisins evenly between the pastry cases, then pour over the filling mixture. Bake in the hot oven for 15–20 minutes until the pastry is cooked and the surface of the tart slightly crisp. Don't be alarmed if the filling seems to come over the top of the cases, as it will sink back down when out of the oven. Allow to cool a little before easing them from the tin. Serve warm or cold.

Ubiquitous in Jamaica, and also found all over the Caribbean, these tropical patties are said to have their roots in the traditional Cornish pasty, thanks to a long colonial history going back centuries. Here, they are made of a tender golden turmeric pastry stuffed with a classic curried minced beef filling. They make a tropical addition to a picnic feast.

JAMAICAN PATTIES

MAKES 8 SNACK-SIZED PATTIES

1 tablespoon olive oil
400g minced beef
2 carrots, finely chopped
1 large onion, finely chopped
1 red pepper, deseeded and finely chopped
2 garlic cloves, crushed
1 teaspoon curry paste
a pinch of dried thyme
1 x 400g can chopped tomatoes
salt and freshly ground black pepper

for the pastry
450g plain flour, plus extra for dusting
1 teaspoon ground turmeric
½ teaspoon fine salt
225g butter, cut into 1cm cubes
about 8 tablespoons ice-cold water

To make the pastry, place the flour, turmeric and salt in a food processor and pulse together briefly. Add the butter and pulse until the mixture looks like coarse breadcrumbs. While pulsing, add just enough ice-cold water to bring the mixture together into loose clumps. You can also make the pastry by hand: rub the dry ingredients and butter together between your fingers and thumbs until it resembles breadcrumbs, then add the water and stir through with a knife to incorporate it, bringing the mixture together with your hands. Place the pastry on a sheet of cling film and draw up the edges, gently pressing it into a ball. Chill in the fridge while you make the filling.

Pour the oil into a deep frying pan and set over a high heat. Add the mince and fry for about 10 minutes or until lightly browned, breaking the clumps up with a wooden spoon as it cooks. Reduce the temperature to medium-low, then add the carrots, onion and red pepper, along with the garlic, curry paste and thyme, and fry for a further 10 minutes, stirring every now and then.

Add the tomatoes along with 150ml cold water and season well with salt and black pepper. Bring to the boil and simmer, uncovered, for around 30 minutes or until the sauce is well reduced, stirring occasionally. Remove from the heat, taste to check the seasoning, adding a little more salt and pepper if necessary, then set aside to cool completely.

Preheat the oven to 200°C/180°C Fan/Gas Mark 6. On a lightly floured work surface, cut the pastry into 8 equal-sized pieces, gently rolling each one into a ball. Roll out each ball into a circle about the size of a large saucer and about 3mm thick. Brush all around the edges with a little cold water and then spoon some filling on to one half of each circle, leaving a generous 1cm border around the edge. For each patty, bring the pastry up and over the filling, pressing down firmly at the edges to completely seal the filling inside. Trim each one with a sharp knife to give you a neat 'D' shape, then take a fork and press down the sealed edge to give you a traditional finish.

Place the patties on a baking tray and bake in the oven for 25 minutes until the pastry is cooked; because of the turmeric, they won't turn golden brown like traditional shortcrust pastry, but should instead be a bright yellow. Serve hot or warm.

Deep, dark and delicious thanks to an intensely aromatic blend of herbs and spices, jerk chicken is perhaps the best-known Jamaican street food. It's always cooked outside, often in old oil barrels converted to grills, and it's pretty much always served with rice and peas – although the 'peas' are actually black beans. This is a recipe to save for a barbecue as it just won't taste the same if cooked in the oven.

Note: you will need to begin this recipe several hours before you want to eat, or even the day before, as the chicken needs time to marinate.

JERK CHICKEN, RICE AND PEAS

SERVES 6

6 large chicken legs
300g rice
1 x 400ml can coconut milk
1 teaspoon allspice berries, bruised, or ½ teaspoon ground allspice
1 tablespoon dried thyme
1 teaspoon dried oregano
1 teaspoon chilli flakes
1 x 400g can black beans, drained
1 lime, cut into wedges
salt and freshly ground black pepper

for the jerk spice paste
4cm piece fresh root ginger, finely grated
3 garlic cloves, crushed
2 Scotch bonnet chillies, finely chopped (seeds removed for less heat)
2 tablespoons vegetable oil
2 tablespoons ground allspice
2 tablespoons ground cinnamon
2 tablespoons paprika
2 tablespoons dried thyme
2 tablespoons soft brown sugar

For the jerk spice paste, place the ginger, garlic, chillies and oil in a small bowl and stir to combine. Add the allspice, cinnamon, paprika, thyme, sugar, salt and pepper, and stir well. Rub the spice paste all over the chicken legs – you may want to wear gloves for this as the chillies are mighty hot! Cover and leave to marinate in the fridge for 2 hours, or preferably overnight.

When you are ready to cook the chicken, light the barbecue. If you are using a gas barbecue, fire up one side to get it really hot; if you are using charcoal, heap the coals to one side to give you a hot side and a cool side. Place the chicken on the hot side and cook for about 10–15 minutes, turning regularly until lightly charred all over. Then move to the cool side of the grill and shut the lid. Leave for 20–30 minutes, until cooked through, turning occasionally – the cooking time very much depends on the temperature of the grill and the size of the chicken legs. It's better to cook low and slow than end up with a charred outside and a raw inside. If you have a meat thermometer, the internal temperature should be 75°C/170°F.

While the chicken is grilling, make the rice and peas. Take a medium-sized saucepan with a snug-fitting lid and add the rice. Pour in the coconut milk and 200ml water and add the allspice, thyme, oregano and chilli. Stir well and leave to soak for 30 minutes.

Stir the black beans through the rice and set over a medium heat. Bring to the boil, clamp on the lid and boil for exactly 1 minute. Turn off the heat, but do not remove the lid. Leave the rice to finish cooking undisturbed for 13 minutes. Remove the lid and fluff lightly with a fork. Season to taste with a little salt and freshly ground black pepper, then serve the chicken alongside the rice and peas with lime wedges on the side.

Bacalaito are pancake-like fritters made with salt cod. They are served all over Puerto Rico, from beaches and roadside stands to fiestas and street parties. With a crisp outside and a dense chewy middle, these are seriously addictive and simply fab when served with a shake of hot sauce.

Note: you will need to begin this recipe up to 24 hours before you want to eat, as the fish needs time to soak.

BACALAITO

MAKES ABOUT 16 FRITTERS, SERVING 4–6

500g salt cod
250g plain flour
1 teaspoon baking powder
1 red or green pepper, finely diced
2 garlic cloves, crushed
a bunch of coriander, chopped
freshly ground black pepper
a little vegetable oil, for frying
hot chilli sauce, to serve

Put the salt cod in a large lidded tub and cover completely with cold water. Leave to soak in the fridge for a minimum of 12 hours, or ideally 24 hours, with a change of water halfway through; this rehydrates the fish and allows some of the salt to soak out.

Drain and discard the water, and lay the fish in a single layer in a deep frying pan. Cover with fresh cold water and set over a medium-high heat. Cover the pan with a lid or snugly fitting piece of kitchen foil and simmer for 15 minutes, by which time the fish should be tender and flake easily with a fork. If it's still a little tough, simmer for a few minutes longer.

Using a fish slice, slide the cooked fish on to a plate and leave to cool a little. Once you can comfortably touch it, flake it into little pieces, carefully discarding all the bones and any skin. Set aside.

Stir the flour and baking powder together into a large bowl and pour in 350ml water, whisking continuously until you have a smooth batter. Stir through the pepper, garlic and coriander and season generously with black pepper. You won't need any extra salt. Finally, fold through the flakes of salt cod and leave to rest for 30 minutes.

Add a drizzle of vegetable oil to a large frying pan and set over a high heat. When the oil is smoking hot, add 1 tablespoonful of mixture per fritter, spread out across the pan, flattening each one as you go. You may need to do this in batches. Fry for 2–3 minutes on one side, then flip over with a fish slice and fry for another 2–3 minutes. Drain over kitchen paper and repeat until you have used up all the mixture.

Serve the *bacalaito* piping hot with the chilli sauce drizzled on top.

An Indian-influenced *chana* (chickpea) curry sandwiched between two pieces of crisp naan-style bread called *bara*, a Trini double is *the* street food to eat in Trinidad after a spot of 'liming' – that's hanging out with music and a few beers to you and me... As with the best post-pub food you can prepare almost everything beforehand, including shaping the dough, so the eating bit can happen quickly. They are messy, but that's just part of the fun!

Note: you will need to begin this recipe the day before you want to eat, as the chickpeas need to soak overnight.

TRINI DOUBLE

MAKES 4 TRINI DOUBLES

200g dried chickpeas
1 teaspoon bicarbonate of soda
1 tablespoon cumin seeds
1 tablespoon coriander seeds
2 tablespoons vegetable oil
1 large onion, chopped
4 garlic cloves, chopped
1 teaspoon ground turmeric
salt and freshly ground black
    pepper
mango chutney, to serve
cucumber, cut into thin
    matchsticks, to serve
hot chilli sauce, to serve

for the bara dough
300g plain flour
1 teaspoon fast-action yeast
1 teaspoon cumin seeds
1 teaspoon ground turmeric
½ teaspoon salt
175–200ml warm water
1 tablespoon vegetable oil, plus
    extra for frying

Soak the chickpeas overnight in plenty of cold water.

To make the dough, place the flour in a large bowl and stir through the yeast, cumin seeds, turmeric and salt. Pour in the water gradually, mixing together until you have a stiff dough; you may not need all the water. Drizzle the oil on to the worktop and tip the dough on to it. Knead in the oil for a few minutes until smooth. Put back in the bowl, cover and leave to prove for about an hour, until doubled in size.

Meanwhile, drain the chickpeas and rinse under plenty of cold water, then tip into a large pan and cover with fresh cold water. Add the bicarbonate of soda and set over a medium heat. Bring to the boil and cook for 25–35 minutes, until tender. Drain and set aside.

Set another large saucepan over a medium heat and add the cumin and coriander seeds. Toast for a minute or so until you can smell their aroma wafting up from the pan. Tip into a spice mill or pestle and mortar and grind to a powder. Set aside.

Set the pan back over a low heat and add the oil. Stir through the onion and gently fry until soft and translucent, about 20 minutes. Add the garlic and ground spices along with the turmeric and fry for another minute. Tip in the cooked chickpeas and 500ml cold water, bring to the boil and simmer steadily until thick and rich, about 30 minutes. Stir regularly and mash up a few of the chickpeas with the back of a wooden spoon. Taste and season with salt and pepper.

Once proved tip the dough on to the worktop and chop into 8 even-sized pieces. Flatten each into a disc 5mm thick and about 12cm in diameter.

Heat a tablespoon of oil in a large frying pan. When it's really hot, add 4 of the *bara* and fry for 2–3 minutes on each side until crisp but not particularly coloured. If the oil is hot enough they will puff up a little. Drain over kitchen paper while you cook the remaining 4.

To assemble the doubles, take 2 *bara* and slightly overlap them on a piece of baking parchment. Spoon a couple of tablespoons of *chana* into the middle, add a dollop of mango chutney, a little cucumber and a shake of chilli sauce to taste. Fold over the *bara* to enclose the filling as best you can, and wrap the parchment around it so it supports the double as you eat.

These deliciously cheesy quesadillas make fabulous party food, and this is an easy recipe to scale up to feed a whole crowd of revellers. Recipe purists should note that traditional Mexican quesadillas are made with one tortilla folded over the filling into a half-moon shape, rather than sandwiching the filling between two tortillas, which is called a *sincronizada* ('synchronised', in Spanish).

CHICKEN AND SWEETCORN QUESADILLAS WITH GUACAMOLE AND SOURED CREAM

MAKES 6 QUESADILLAS

1 tablespoon cumin seeds
1 teaspoon dried chilli flakes
1 teaspoon olive oil, plus extra
  for frying
3 garlic cloves, chopped
4 spring onions, finely sliced
4 medium tomatoes, chopped
1 x 325g can sweetcorn, drained
350g mature Cheddar cheese,
  grated
250g cooked chicken, chopped
a bunch of coriander, chopped
6 large soft flour tortillas
salt and freshly ground black
  pepper
soured cream, to serve

for the guacamole
2 large ripe avocados, stones
  removed and flesh scooped
  out
juice of ½ lime
1 garlic clove, crushed
1 tablespoon olive oil
a few drops of hot chilli sauce,
  to taste

Set a small frying pan over a medium-high heat and add the cumin seeds and chilli flakes. Toast for a minute or so until you can smell their aroma wafting up from the pan. Add the olive oil and garlic, stirring briefly for just 30 seconds before adding the spring onions and tomatoes. Season well with plenty of black pepper and a little salt and fry for a couple of minutes until the tomatoes start to soften. Tip into a large bowl and stir through the sweetcorn, cheese, chicken and coriander.

Assemble the quesadillas by taking 1 tortilla and spooning a layer of filling, about 2cm deep, over one half. Fold over the other half to completely enclose the filling and give you the half-moon shape. Repeat with the remaining 5 tortillas. The assembled quesadillas can be kept in the fridge for a few hours, if you like. Alternatively, the filling can be chilled for up to 2 days before assembly.

To make the guacamole, place the avocado flesh in a deep jug. Add the lime juice, garlic, olive oil, chilli sauce to taste and a little salt and pepper. Pulse with a stick blender until smooth, or mash with a fork for a chunkier guacamole.

When you are ready to cook, set a large non-stick frying pan over a medium-high heat and drizzle in a teaspoon of olive oil. Scrunch up a piece of kitchen paper and spread the oil into a very thin layer. Once the oil is hot, add one of the quesadillas and fry for about 90 seconds on each side, turning with a fish slice until they are crisp and the cheese is melted. Repeat with the remaining quesadillas. Slice each one into wedges and serve with the guacamole and a dollop of soured cream on top or on the side.

Mexican *tamales* are lovely parcels of steamed corn dough stuffed with a variety of usually meaty fillings. I've used a seductive mix of pulled pork and punchy chilli sauce. Making tamales is a little labour-intensive, but you can make the pork and sauce ahead of time, and it will keep in the fridge very happily for a day or two.

TAMALES WITH PULLED PORK AND CHILLI SAUCE

MAKES 12 TAMALES, SERVING 6–8

3 tomatoes, roughly chopped
1 large onion, roughly chopped
5 garlic cloves, roughly chopped
1 tablespoon cumin seeds, toasted
1 teaspoon dried chilli flakes
1.2kg belly pork
60g whole dried chillies, about 5–6 large ones (I use a mixture of dried guajillo and mulato chillies)
salt and freshly ground black pepper

for the tamales
300g masa harina
2 teaspoons baking powder
½ teaspoon fine salt
75g butter, melted
around 300ml hot chicken or vegetable stock

you will need
15 dry corn husks, the wider the better

Preheat the oven to 160°C/140°C Fan/Gas Mark 3. Place the tomatoes, onion, garlic, cumin and chilli flakes in a food processor, along with a good seasoning of salt and pepper, and purée until smooth.

Place the pork belly, skin side up, in a small roasting tin – it should fit quite snugly – and pour over the tomato sauce, spreading it all over the meat. Cover the tin tightly with a double layer of kitchen foil and slow-roast in the oven for about 3½ hours. The meat should be so tender that you can tease it apart with a fork. If it's not quite there, re-cover and cook for a further 30 minutes or so.

Remove the foil and carefully strain out the cooking juices into a saucepan. Increase the oven temperature to 200°C/180°C Fan/Gas Mark 6 and put the pork back in, uncovered, for another 30 minutes to give it a little colour all over.

Place the chillies on a baking tray and slide it into the oven alongside the pork for just 3 minutes or so. You want to toast them so they are deeply coloured all over; they will be slightly blackened and crispy. Remove from the oven, pull off and discard the stalks and add the chillies to the pan of reserved cooking juices. Top up with 250ml cold water, pressing the chillies under the surface as much as you can. Cover the pan and simmer over a low heat for 20 minutes to rehydrate the chillies. Tip into a blender and purée until smooth, then pass through a sieve into a clean bowl, discarding the seeds and membranes of the chillies. Place half the sauce in a second bowl and set aside to serve as a sauce to go with the tamales.

Remove the pork from the oven and transfer to a plate to cool a little. Once it's cool enough to handle, remove and discard the skin and shred the meat with your fingers, tossing it into the first bowl of sauce as you go. Remove as much fat as you want to, but I'd urge you to not be too vigilant as a little fat will add much in the way of juicy succulence.

Place the corn husks in a large bowl or saucepan and pour over enough boiling water to cover well. Leave to soak for an hour or so; they need to be nice and pliable for rolling. Drain and pat dry. Take 3 husks and tear down the length to form long, thin strips – these will be used to tie up the tamales.

For the tamales, add the masa harina to a bowl and stir through the baking powder and salt. Add the melted butter, then start to pour in the stock, stirring constantly until you have a smooth, pliable dough. You may not need all the stock, or you may need a splash more (hot water is fine if you need a little extra liquid). Knead briefly to make sure it's evenly mixed, then divide the dough into 12 even pieces, rolling each into a ball.

To assemble the tamales, take a whole rehydrated corn husk and lay it on the worktop, wide end towards you. Put one of the balls of masa dough in the centre and flatten it out over the husk in a rough rectangle about 4–5mm thick, ensuring you have a generous 2cm border of uncovered husk all round. The thinner you can get the masa the better, as it swells on cooking.

Take a tablespoon or so of pork filling and lay it down the centre of the masa. Roll up the sides over the filling, drawing the masa dough together at the top so you have a sausage shape of dough with a line of pork along the inside. Roll the sides up and tuck in the ends to form a neat parcel. Use the torn strips of husk, one at each end, to tie it into a neat parcel. Repeat with the remaining 11 whole husks. Uncooked tamales freeze very well at this point: place them on a baking tray to freeze initially, then pack into a bag or tub and leave in the freezer until ready to cook.

Add the tamales to a large steamer basket in a couple of layers. Pour boiling water into a pan to just under the level of the steamer and set over a medium heat. Cover with a tight-fitting lid and steam for an hour, checking the level of water every now and then and topping up as necessary. If cooking from frozen, cook for a few minutes longer.

Serve the tamales in the husks for people to unwrap, with the reserved chilli sauce alongside.

Fish tacos are often found in the Baja California region of Mexico. However, they aren't as common across the US and abroad, so I decided to share a little bit of Baja California with you in this recipe. What makes these tacos Ensendada-style is the unique sour cream sauce that is made in this port town on the Pacific. Crack open a beer, squeeze some fresh lime and be transported to Mexico!

TACOS DE PESCADO ESTILO ENSENADA

 Claudia Sandoval
MasterChef USA, 2015 Champion

MAKES 16 TACOS

900g skinless red snapper fillets
sea salt
16 corn tortillas
200g shredded white cabbage
chopped red chilli, to garnish
chopped coriander, to garnish
lime wedges

for the Ensenada-style soured cream
125g soured cream
6 tablespoons mayonnaise
2 tablespoons lime juice
1 tablespoon cold water
salt and freshly ground black
    pepper, to taste

for the dry dredge
100g plain flour
1 teaspoon salt
1 teaspoon freshly ground black
    pepper
1 teaspoon granulated garlic

for the fish batter
300g plain flour
1½ teaspoons salt
¼ teaspoon freshly ground
    black pepper
¼ teaspoon paprika
1 teaspoon granulated garlic
2 large eggs
500ml lager-style beer

To make the soured cream, place all the ingredients in a bowl and whisk until completely incorporated and a little runny, but not watery. If it's too runny, add a little more sour cream and mayonnaise to balance the thickness. Refrigerate until ready to use.

To make the dry dredge, place all the ingredients in a shallow bowl and whisk to incorporate.

For the fish batter, combine the flour, salt, pepper, paprika and granulated garlic in a large shallow bowl. Whisk in the eggs and beer. The mixture should be the consistency of pancake batter. If it is too thick, add a little cold water to thin it out.

Heat the oil in a deep fat fryer to 190°C/375°F. Prepare to fry the fish by setting a cooling rack over a baking sheet to drain any residual fat (if you don't have a cooling rack, kitchen paper set over a flat plate will work too). One at a time, add the red snapper fillets to the dry dredge and toss to coat. Transfer to a plate or baking tray. Working in batches, dredge the fish into the batter, allowing the excess to drip off, and carefully place them in the deep fat fryer. Fry for 3–5 minutes, flipping them once the underside is browned, until golden brown on both sides. Remove to the wire rack to drain and immediately sprinkle with sea salt.

While the fish is frying, preheat a frying pan over a high heat until nice and hot. Lower the heat and cook the tortillas for about a minute on each side, until malleable, placing them in a tea towel as they are done to keep them warm.

To serve, place a piece of fried fish on each tortilla, top with shredded cabbage and soured cream, and garnish with the red chilli and coriander. Serve with the lime wedges alongside.

Nieve means 'snow' in Spanish, and this is a boozy, fruity grown-up sorbet popular on street food carts across Mexico. It is such a simple, easy treat, perfect for sharing on hot days. The double blitzing in the food processor makes it very smooth, and it just melts on your tongue.

Note: you will need to begin this recipe several hours before you want to eat, or even the day before, as the sorbet needs time to freeze.

TEQUILA, MANGO AND LIME NIEVE

SERVES 4–6

2 large ripe mangoes, flesh
   chopped
juice of 3 limes
200g agave nectar or golden
   syrup
100ml tequila
lime zest, to garnish

Place the mango flesh in a food processor and blitz to a purée. Add the lime juice, agave nectar or syrup and tequila and process until smooth. Pour into a shallow tub, cover with a tight-fitting lid and pop in the freezer for several hours or overnight, until frozen.

Once frozen, scrape the sorbet into the clean food processor and blitz again to a smooth, creamy slush. Return to the tub and re-freeze for another hour or two until it's the desired consistency: you can serve it hard like a sorbet, or softer like a slush – it's up to you. Serve in little glasses or mini ice cream tubs, garnished with the lime zest.

Pupusas are thick corn cakes stuffed with cheese, beans or meat. In their home country of El Salvador they are a common sight on street carts or in the fabulously named *pupuserías*, the cafés dedicated to serving them. *Curtido* is a pickled slaw that gets better with time, so make it well ahead for the best possible flavour.

Note: you will need to begin this recipe the day before you want to eat, to allow the flavours of the *curtido* to develop.

PUPUSAS CON CURTIDO

MAKES 8 PUPUSAS, SERVING ABOUT 4

for the curtido
½ white cabbage, finely shredded
1 large carrot, grated
1 small onion, very finely chopped
2 teaspoons coriander seeds
1 teaspoon cumin seeds
75ml cider vinegar
2 teaspoons granulated sugar
1 teaspoon dried oregano
1–2 teaspoons chilli flakes, to taste
salt and freshly ground black pepper

for the refried beans
2 teaspoons cumin seeds
2 tablespoons olive oil
1 onion, finely chopped
2 garlic cloves, crushed
½–1 teaspoon dried chilli flakes
1 x 400g can pinto beans, drained and rinsed

for the pupusas
400g masa harina
60g butter, melted
450–500ml warm water
250g mozzarella, finely diced
vegetable oil, for frying

Begin by making the *curtido* as it needs time to pickle – overnight is ideal, or for a minimum of 6 hours. It will keep in the fridge, maturing nicely, for at least a week, so you can make it well ahead if you want to. Stir together the cabbage, carrot and onion in a large bowl, and season with salt and pepper.

Add the coriander and cumin seeds to a small frying pan and toast over a medium heat for a minute or two. Tip into a spice mill or pestle and mortar and grind to a powder, then add to a saucepan along with the vinegar, 75ml water, sugar, oregano and chilli flakes. Set over a medium heat and bring to the boil, then pour this mix over the vegetables and stir thoroughly. Leave to pickle for as long as possible, stirring every now and then.

For the refried beans, toast the cumin seeds in a dry frying pan over a medium heat for a minute or two. Tip into a pestle and mortar and grind roughly. Pour the oil into the pan and set back over the heat. Once hot and reduced slightly, add the onion and fry for about 15 minutes until soft and lightly coloured. Stir through the garlic, crushed cumin seeds and chilli flakes, and season with salt and pepper. Fry for another minute before tipping in the beans. Cook for about 5 minutes over a medium-low heat, crushing the beans with a potato masher as they heat through. Set aside to cool a little so you can handle them comfortably.

To make the *pupusas*, mix together the masa harina with a generous seasoning of salt and pepper in a bowl. Pour in the melted butter and enough warm water to form a crumbly dough when combined. Tip on to the worktop and knead briefly to bring it together in a ball. Divide into 8 pieces, weighing each for accuracy if you want to ensure even-sized *pupusas*. Take a piece of dough and roll it into a neat compact ball between your palms. Cupping it in one palm, press the thumb of your other hand firmly into the centre to make a hole. Then, working around, gradually enlarge the hole with your thumb and forefinger so you get a deep cup shape.

Supporting the cup in the palm of your hand, take a tablespoon of mozzarella and drop it into the middle. Then add a heaped teaspoon of refried beans on top, pressing it down with the back of the teaspoon. The trick is to get as much filling as possible inside but still be able to seal it up completely. Continue to cup in the palm of your hand as you use the other hand to pinch the sides to meet each other over the filling, completely sealing it in. Then cup in both hands and gently roll into a ball before slowly increasing the pressure, flattening the ball to a disc about 1.5cm thick. If you go slowly and carefully not too many cracks should appear, and if they do, simply push the edges back together. Repeat with the remaining pieces of dough. You will not need to use all the refried beans, but they will keep for 3–4 days in the fridge (and are fabulous spread on hot buttered toast!).

When you are ready to cook, add a good glug of vegetable oil to a large frying pan – you need a thin layer to cover the base. Set over a high heat and, once hot, fry the *pupusas* a few at a time for about 2 minutes on each side until crisp and golden. Remove from the pan and drain on kitchen paper. Repeat with the remaining *pupusas*, adding a little more oil if necessary. Top each with a little of the *curtido* and eat while still hot.

Arepas are unassuming little cornmeal cakes, but one bite will have you hooked – their crunchy outside and chewy inside make for an addictive texture. They are found all over Venezuela, stuffed full of various tasty fillings, but here I've used my favourite combination of fresh homemade cheese and the wonderfully named *guasacaca*. Guasacaca is an avocado-based sauce, the Venezuelan equivalent of guacamole but with a much more punchy flavour. White cornmeal is different from yellow cornmeal (commonly known as polenta), and it can be a touch tricky to find; try Afro-Caribbean shops or online.

Note: you will need to begin this recipe about 4–5 hours before you want to eat, or even the day before, as the cheese needs time to drain and chill.

AREPAS WITH QUESO BLANCO AND GUASACACA

MAKES 8 AREPAS, SERVING 4–8

for the queso blanco
2 litres whole milk
75ml white wine vinegar
2 teaspoons salt
1 tablespoon cumin seeds, toasted
2–3 jalapeño chillies, finely chopped

for the arepas
500g pre-cooked white cornmeal
2 teaspoons salt
3 tablespoons vegetable or olive oil, plus a little extra for frying
500ml lukewarm water

for the guasacaca
2 large ripe avocados, stones removed and flesh scooped out
2 green peppers, deseeded and roughly chopped
5 spring onions, roughly chopped
3 garlic cloves, chopped
a bunch of flat-leaf parsley
a bunch of coriander
3–4 tablespoons red wine vinegar, to taste
100ml olive oil
salt and freshly ground black pepper

you will need
a clean muslin cloth or cheesecloth to strain the cheese

For the *queso blanco*, pour the milk into a large saucepan or stockpot. Set over a medium-low heat and gently bring up to a little under boiling point (85°C/185°F is perfect if you have a thermometer), stirring occasionally. Turn off the heat and pour in the vinegar, about a third at a time, stirring well between each splash. Leave to rest undisturbed for 5 minutes, by which time you should have a pan of curds and whey.

Line a sieve with a clean muslin cloth or cheesecloth and place over a large bowl or saucepan. Gently pour the curds and whey into the sieve, pausing if necessary to discard the whey as and when the bowl fills up – there will be a lot of liquid.

Leave to drain for a few minutes until the curds stop dripping, and discard any liquid in the bowl. Add the salt, cumin and chillies, and lightly fork through the curds to mix. Draw up the sides of the muslin and twist tightly to form a ball, squeezing a little as you go to press out any remaining moisture. Leave to cool, then transfer the muslin ball of *queso blanco* to a clean bowl and chill in the fridge for several hours or overnight.

To make the *arepas*, place the cornmeal and salt in a large bowl and stir well to mix. Add the oil, and gradually pour in the water, stirring continuously to create a stiff dough. Leave to rest for 30 minutes.

For the *guasacaca*, put all the ingredients except the olive oil into a food processor and whizz until really smooth. With the motor running, trickle the olive oil in slowly. Check the seasoning, adding salt and pepper to taste. Cover with a layer of cling film pressed to the surface and chill until needed.

Tip the *arepas* dough on to the worktop, knead briefly, and then divide the dough into 8 even pieces. Roll each piece into a ball before flattening out to a disc about 1cm thick.

Add a drizzle of oil to a large frying pan and set over a medium heat. Add 4 *arepas* to the pan and cover with a snug-fitting piece of kitchen foil, cooking for about 6–8 minutes until golden brown. Flip over and cook for 6–8 minutes on the other side, uncovered. Keep warm while you repeat with the remaining 4 *arepas*.

To serve, split the *arepas* partway through the middle (as though you were opening up a pitta bread) and fill with the *queso blanco* and a dollop of *guasacaca*.

Coxinha means 'little thigh', and these delicious Brazilian chicken and cream cheese stuffed *croquetas* are vaguely chicken-thigh-shaped. They are a little time-consuming and fiddly to make, so this recipe makes a generous quantity. You can also prepare the filling and dough ahead of time and store in the fridge for up to 24 hours before you shape them, thus spreading the work out a little.

COXINHAS DE GALINHA

MAKES 16 COXINHAS, SERVING ABOUT 8

50g unsalted butter
1 tablespoon vegetable oil
2 onions, finely diced
2 garlic cloves, crushed
1 carrot, finely diced
500ml chicken stock
2 bay leaves
400g chicken thigh fillets
180g cream cheese
grated zest and juice of 1 lime
salt and freshly ground black
    pepper

for the dough
a large pinch of salt
500g plain flour
2 eggs, lightly beaten
150g fine breadcrumbs

Place the butter and oil in a deep saucepan and set it over a medium-low heat to melt. Add the onion and cook gently for around 20 minutes, until soft but not coloured. Add the garlic and fry for a further minute. Scoop out half the onion mixture into a large bowl and set aside to cool.

Add the carrot to the remaining onion in the pan and fry for a further 10 minutes before pouring in the stock and adding the bay leaves. Bring to the boil, then reduce the heat to low and add the chicken thigh fillets, pressing them under the surface as best you can. Cover with a lid and simmer steadily for around 20 minutes, until the chicken is cooked through.

While the chicken is cooking, mix the cream cheese, lime juice and zest through the cooled cooked onion and season well with salt and pepper.

Once the chicken is cooked, remove to a plate to cool a little, reserving the stock, then shred the meat into pieces and set aside to until cold. Once cold, add to the bowl with the cream cheese and onion mixture, stirring well to combine.

For the dough, strain the chicken stock through a fine sieve into a measuring jug, and top up with cold water until you have 500ml again. Pour the stock into a clean pan, add a good pinch of salt and bring to the boil. Once it's simmering steadily, gradually add the flour, stirring constantly until you have a really stiff dough. Tip on to a clean worktop and allow to cool for 15 minutes or so, until you can knead it without burning your hands. Knead for about 5 minutes until smooth. Roll into a ball, wrap in cling film and leave to cool completely. Once cold, chill in the fridge for an hour (longer is fine).

To form the *coxinhas*, cut the dough into 16 even-sized pieces. I find the easiest way to do this is to cut the ball in half, then half again, and so on – the dough should be firm but still malleable. Roll each piece into a ball, then, using a rolling pin, flatten them into discs about 10cm in diameter and 5mm thick. Take a generous teaspoon of the filling and place in the centre of one disc, then draw the sides up and over the filling so they meet at the top like a little purse. Pinch and squeeze the top to form a point; it should look like a little fat pear. Place on a baking tray and repeat with the remaining dough and filling.

Line up the beaten egg in one bowl and the breadcrumbs in another. Dip each *coxinha* into the egg to coat all over, then roll in the breadcrumbs. Repeat until they are all coated in breadcrumbs.

Preheat the oil in a deep fat fryer to 170°C/340°F and fry in batches until crisp and a deep golden colour, about 6–7 minutes per batch. Serve while still hot.

The national dish of Peru, and a popular street-eat all along the coast (and around inland waters, too), ceviche is incredibly easy to make. Prepare your fish in one bowl, the marinating ingredients in another, then once you mix the two together it takes just 10 minutes to 'cook' the fish to perfection.

CEVICHE

SERVES 6–8

400g sea bass fillets (as fresh as you can find), cut into 1cm cubes
1 teaspoon salt
juice of 5 fat limes
½ red onion, very finely sliced
3 or 4 hot red chillies (e.g. bird's eye), finely chopped
a small bunch of coriander, chopped
freshly ground black pepper
a drizzle of olive oil, to serve

Place the diced fish in a bowl. Sprinkle over the salt, stirring well to mix. Leave to rest for 5 minutes.

In a separate bowl or jug, mix together the lime juice, onion, chillies, coriander and a good grind of black pepper.

About 10 minutes before you want to serve, simply pour the marinade over the fish, stir well, and leave to rest. To serve, spoon into small cups or pile on a plate and drizzle over a little olive oil.

In Argentina, the *asado*, or barbecue, is taken very seriously indeed, but the meat cooked is treated simply, usually seasoned with salt alone, so the quality of the beef is paramount. In this recipe I use 'English cut' beef short ribs, which are best cooked low and slow over an indirect heat. With each rib, you get a short section of bone with a thick chunk of meat attached to one side. Chimichurri is the quintessential Argentinian *asado* sauce, generously poured over pretty much everything that comes off the grill. It's like a really punchy pesto, zingy with vinegar, lemons and plenty of garlic.

SLOW-GRILLED SHORT RIBS WITH CHIMICHURRI SAUCE

SERVES 4–6

2kg beef short ribs, cut into individual ribs
3 teaspoons sea salt flakes

for the chimichurri sauce
a large bunch of flat-leaf parsley, larger stalks discarded
1 generous tablespoon of oregano or marjoram leaves
3 garlic cloves
1 tablespoon red wine vinegar
½ teaspoon dried chilli flakes
juice of ½ lemon
125ml olive oil
salt and freshly ground black pepper

If you are using a gas barbecue, light half the burners, ideally one at either end of the grill, leaving the middle section off. If you are using a charcoal grill, light a big mound of coals (you need the fire to be gently alight for 3 hours so use plenty). Once the coals are white-hot, push them to one side of the grill, leaving the other side coal-free.

Spread the ribs out in a sturdy roasting tin and sprinkle liberally with sea salt flakes, then turn the ribs so they all face bone down, meat up. Set the tin on the cool area of the charcoal grill, or over the unlit burners of the gas grill. Close the lid and cook for 3 hours, checking every now and then and turning the tin as necessary to make sure the ribs are cooking evenly. This is more important if you are using charcoal as the heat will all be coming from one side. If your barbecue has a thermometer on the lid you are aiming to keep the interior temperature at around 200–220°C/400–425°F. The ribs are ready when the meat is deep and dark and starting to come away from the bone.

To make the chimichurri sauce, roughly tear the parsley and add it to a food processor, along with the oregano or marjoram. Pulse until finely chopped. Add the garlic, red wine vinegar, chilli flakes, lemon juice and a generous seasoning of salt and pepper. Blitz to a purée. With the motor running, trickle in the olive oil in a steady stream. Once it's well mixed, taste to check the seasoning, adding more salt, pepper, chilli or lemon, to taste. It should be punchy! Scrape into a bowl and leave at room temperature while the short ribs are cooking.

Serve the ribs with the sauce alongside to drizzle over as you eat.

Garrapiñada are delicious caramelised nuts made in large shallow copper pans by street vendors of Argentina and Uruguay. They are usually piled into cellophane cones to serve and make a great little edible gift. They are often made with peanuts instead of almonds – just make sure you use unsalted nuts with the skins on, as the caramel doesn't stick well to skinless nuts.

GARRAPIÑADA ALMENDRAS

SERVES 8, AS A TREAT

400g almonds or unsalted
   peanuts (skin on)
400g caster sugar
400ml water
1 tablespoon vanilla extract

Place all the ingredients in a heavy-based saucepan set over a medium heat and bring to the boil. Reduce the heat to a steady simmer and cook for about 30 minutes until the sugar syrup has thickened and reduced, stirring occasionally. Once the liquid has nearly gone, the sugar will start to crystallise.

Continue to cook over a medium-low heat for a further 8–10 minutes, stirring frequently, until the nuts are nicely coated with crystallised sugar. Keep a very close eye on the pan towards the end of the cooking time as the molten sugar turns crystalline in a flash; the cooking time will vary a little depending on the surface area of your chosen pan.

Tip on to a sheet of baking parchment and spread out in a single layer to cool. Once cold, pack into cellophane bags or cones, or store in an airtight jar. They will keep for several weeks in an airtight container.

If there's one thing Argentinians love more than a juicy steak it's the uber sweet *dulce de leche*, an intensely creamy, thick caramel sauce. You can buy it ready made, but you just can't beat the flavour of homemade. The secret to success is to cook it really, really slowly, so you need to commit yourself to 3 or 4 patient hours or more in the kitchen. If you do it too quickly, you risk the milk proteins curdling, leaving you with a gritty end result. This recipe makes more *dulce de leche* than you need for the ice cream, but it will keep in the fridge for at least a month, and is fabulous spread on to hot waffles (see page 72) or toast.

Note: you will need to begin this recipe the day before you want to eat, as the *dulce de leche* needs to be chilled thoroughly before turning into ice cream; the ice cream itself takes at least another 5–6 hours to freeze.

DULCE DE LECHE ICE CREAM

SERVES 6–8

2 litres whole milk
600g granulated sugar
1 teaspoon bicarbonate of soda
600ml whipping cream
2 teaspoons vanilla extract
a few pecans, crushed, to
    garnish

Pour about 500ml of the milk into a large saucepan or stockpot and set it over a medium heat. Add the sugar and stir continuously until it has dissolved. Then pour in the rest of the milk and add the bicarbonate of soda, stirring until completely mixed.

Reduce the heat to an absolute minimum and leave to caramelise for about 3½ hours. Give the mixture a stir from time to time, about every 15 minutes or so. You are looking to keep it from boiling, just at a bare simmer, or you will be in danger of a grainy, rather than smooth, result.

Turn off the heat when the *dulce de leche* is a deep caramel bronze and about the consistency of thick double cream. It will thicken to a spreadable consistency once cold. If in doubt, put a little on a spoon and chill quickly in the fridge to check what it will be like when cold. This recipe should yield around 500–600ml *dulce de leche*. Pour 400ml into a jug and set aside to go cold, then chill thoroughly. This will be the base for the ice cream. Store the rest in a jar or covered bowl in the fridge to be used as desired.

When you are ready to make the ice cream, pour the cream into a large bowl and add the vanilla extract. Whisk to firm peaks by hand or using an electric whisk, then take a large metal spoon and fold through the measured chilled *dulce de leche*.

Pour into a plastic tub, cover and put in the freezer for at least 5–6 hours, or overnight, until set. To serve, remove from the freezer and allow to sit at room temperature for 30 minutes before scooping into cups or cones.

EUROPE

With the climate of Europe spanning the often-baking hot Mediterranean to the sometimes positively chilly northern countries, it's hardly surprising that street food on this continent is equally eclectic. Naturally, with colder weather the food on the street veers more towards comfort than speed, such as Anders Halskov-Jensen's *biksemad* recipe, and Northern Europe excels at deep-fried delights and oozing melted cheese, whilst in the south things tend to be smaller, snackier and lighter – little miniature meatballs with a punchy tomato sauce, or the fresh niçoise salad wraps from the French Riviera, or Italy's world-famous gelato.

As a continent, Europe perhaps has embraced the trend of street eating as a social event more than any other, with specialised food markets popping up all over the place. Germany's world-famous Christmas markets sum up all that is good about eating on the street whilst wrapped in a snuggly coat – from crisp potato and apple fritters to dairy heavy pizzas or decadent fruit and cream laden waffles, all best washed down with warming spicy gluwein! Meanwhile crêperies are a familiar sight all across France, and offer inspiration for Marc Boissieux's take on a banoffee crêpe.

It's never been easier to find food from all corners of the globe in Europe, but there are also plenty of indigenous specialities that are hard to beat, including Simon Wood's masterful take on a British pub classic, the humble but delectable Scotch egg, and Luca Manfè's classic Italian bar snack, *gnocco fritto*.

My black pudding Scotch eggs are a great snack, and this classic combination of flavours are great served with a good mayonnaise or piccalilli, and of course are excellent when washed down with a good beer! They're delicious warm, but are just as good cold at any time of day.

BLACK PUDDING SCOTCH EGGS

 Simon Wood,
MasterChef UK, 2015 Champion

SERVES 6

600g Bury black pudding
75g fresh white breadcrumbs
7 medium free-range eggs
1 tablespoon chopped oregano
vegetable or sunflower oil, for frying
salt and freshly ground black pepper

for the panne (breadcrumb) coating
100g plain flour
2 medium free-range eggs
200g coarse fresh white breadcrumbs
1 teaspoon dried oregano

Place the black pudding, breadcrumbs, 1 egg and the oregano into a bowl. Using a fork, break down the black pudding and combine the ingredients evenly, season generously with salt and pepper and divide the mixture into 6 equal portions.

Bring a saucepan of water just to the boil, add the 6 eggs and cook for 6 minutes, which will give you a soft, creamy yellow yolk. Place the saucepan into the sink and run the cold tap over the eggs until they are cool, then remove the shells.

Use your hands to flatten one of the portions of black pudding into a rough disc, about 10–12cm in diameter, depending on the size of your eggs. Place a boiled egg in the centre and carefully shape the black pudding evenly around the egg, making sure to seal the joins well. Repeat this process with the remaining black pudding and eggs.

For the panne coating, set out 3 bowls. Put the flour into one bowl and season it with salt and pepper. Whisk the eggs into another bowl, and place the breadcrumbs and dried oregano into the final bowl.

Lightly coat each Scotch egg with the seasoned flour, then place it into the beaten egg, then roll it in the breadcrumbs. I like to repeat the egg and breadcrumb stages to get a thick, crunchy coating on my egg. Reshape the eggs so they are perfectly round, if required, then place them in the fridge to firm up.

Take a large saucepan and heat 15cm of oil to 175°C/345°F, or use a deep fat fryer if you have one. It's hot enough when a 1cm square of bread turns golden in about a minute. Carefully place 2 or 3 eggs at a time into the oil; if you overload the pan the temperature of the oil will drop and you will end up with soggy eggs that stick together! Cook for 6–8 minutes, turning regularly to ensure that they are evenly golden and crisp. Drain on kitchen paper and serve.

Coming from Cornwall, I have a real weakness for a properly seasoned Cornish pasty, although to my mind they taste their best when eaten by the sea accompanied by the sound of seagulls! The pastry here is unusual because it's made with strong bread flour, which results in a sturdier crust to support the robust filling.

CORNISH PASTIES

MAKES 8 PASTIES

400g beef skirt, cut into 1cm cubes
400g waxy potatoes, peeled and cut into 1cm cubes
300g swede, peeled and cut into 1cm cubes
1 onion, chopped
a little butter
1 egg, lightly beaten
salt and freshly ground black pepper, plus extra sea salt flakes for sprinkling (optional)

for the pastry
600g strong white bread flour
150g butter, cut into 1cm cubes
150g lard or vegetable shortening, cut into 1cm cubes
1 teaspoon fine salt
about 16–18 tablespoons ice-cold water

To make the pastry, add the flour, butter, lard or shortening and salt to a large bowl and stir together until the fats are completely coated in flour. Gradually add just enough ice-cold water to bring it together into a firm dough that is not too sticky. There should be no loose pieces of fat or flour left in the bowl.

Turn on to a lightly floured work surface and roll into a rectangle about 1cm thick. With the shorter edge facing you, fold the top third towards you into the middle, and the bottom third up and over it, just like folding a letter. Turn the pastry by 90 degrees, roll out again to a 1cm-thick rectangle and repeat the folding, adding a little more flour as necessary to stop it from sticking. Repeat this turning, rolling and folding process 4 or 5 times. Wrap tightly in cling film and chill for an hour.

To make the filling, combine the beef, potato, swede and onion in a large bowl and season generously with salt and pepper. Cover and set aside while the pastry chills.

Preheat the oven to 200°C/180°C Fan/Gas Mark 6. On a lightly floured worktop, cut the pastry into 8 even-sized pieces. Shape into a ball and then roll each piece out to a circle about 5mm thick. Add a little pile of cooled filling to one half of each circle, leaving a generous 2cm margin around the edge. Bring the empty half of the pastry up and over the filling, encasing it completely. Press the edges of the pastry together, then twist along like a rope to crimp and seal. Brush with a little beaten egg and scatter over a few flakes of sea salt, if you fancy.

Spread the pasties over two baking trays and put into the hot oven. Reduce the heat to 180°C/160°C Fan/Gas Mark 4 and bake for 45 minutes until deep golden brown. Best served steaming hot from the oven.

Good old fish and chips is the ultimate British street food, ideally eaten by the seaside on a blustery day! Triple-cooked chips are a bit of an effort, but they are worth it – the chilling in the fridge guarantees a supreme crunch. And if you are making chips, you may as well make plenty, so this recipe gives a generous portion each.

FISH AND CHIPS WITH PROPER TARTARE SAUCE

SERVES 4

1.2kg floury potatoes, ideally Maris Piper
100g plain flour
100g cornflour
1 teaspoon ground turmeric
1 teaspoon fine salt
800g firm white fish fillet (cod, haddock, ling or pollack), ideally 2–3cm thick
200ml ice-cold beer (golden ale or lager)
lemon wedges, to serve
sea salt flakes

for the tartare sauce
2 egg yolks
1 teaspoon Dijon mustard
½ teaspoon salt
175ml neutral-tasting oil such as groundnut
25ml olive oil
juice of ½ lemon
50g cornichons, finely chopped
2 tablespoons chopped flat-leaf parsley
1 tablespoon capers, finely chopped
1 shallot, finely chopped
salt and freshly ground black pepper

Peel the potatoes and slice into 1cm-thick chips. Place in a colander and rinse well under cold running water. Tip into a large saucepan and shake in a little sea salt. Pour in enough boiling water to submerge the chips and cover with a lid. Bring back to the boil and cook until just tender when pierced with the tip of a sharp knife, about 3–4 minutes. Drain well and spread out on a large baking tray to steam dry. Leave to go completely cold.

Heat the oil in a deep fat fryer to 120°C/250°F. Fry the parboiled chips for about 5 minutes until soft all the way through but not coloured at all. You may need to do this in 2 or 3 batches depending on the size of your fryer. Drain thoroughly then spread out once again on a baking tray in a single layer. Leave to go cold then chill in the fridge for a few hours, or preferably overnight.

Make the tartare sauce by placing the egg yolks, mustard and salt in the bowl of a food mixer. Using the whisk attachment, whizz until smooth and completely combined. Measure the oils into a jug, then, with the motor running, start to add the oils very slowly, literally drop by drop at first, letting the sauce whizz and mix between each addition. If you go too fast you risk separation rather than emulsification. Once the egg is thickening and turning paler you can increase the flow of oil to a few drops at a time, very gradually increasing to a thin trickle as it begins to look like mayonnaise. When all the oil is in, add the lemon juice and whisk once more until combined. Then fold through the cornichons, parsley, capers and shallot with a tablespoon. Taste to check the seasoning, adding black pepper, extra salt or a squeeze more lemon to taste before scooping into a bowl and chilling until needed (overnight is fine).

For the batter, mix the plain flour, cornflour, turmeric and salt together in a large bowl. Cut the fish into 4 even-sized pieces and lay on a large plate or baking tray. Take a generous tablespoon of the seasoned flour and sprinkle it over the fish, then toss the fish around to get a light, even coating. Gradually pour the beer into the remaining flour in the bowl, whisking all the time until you have a smooth batter.

Preheat the oven to 140°C/120°C Fan/Gas Mark 1 so you can keep the fish warm while the chips are cooking. Heat the oil in the deep fat fryer to 180°C/350°F.

Have the plate of fish and bowl of batter right next to the deep fat fryer. Dip a piece of fish into the batter, completely submerging it so it gets an even coating, then immediately slide it gently into the hot oil. Repeat with another piece of fish and leave both to fry for about 5 minutes, until the batter is golden and puffed up. Drain briefly over kitchen paper and slide into the warm oven on a baking tray while you repeat with the remaining 2 pieces. Slide those into the oven too, to keep warm while you give the chips their final crisping in the fryer.

Fry the chips for a second time – at the higher heat of 180°C/350°F – again in batches if necessary, until golden and really crisp, about 4 minutes. Drain briefly before scattering over a little sea salt and serving immediately with the fish and the tartare sauce with lemon wedges on the side.

These traditional waffles are a street staple in their native Belgium. Unlike American waffles (which use baking powder), these have a little yeast in the batter. The result is a light and airy inside and a crisp outside. As to what to top your waffle with – the world is your oyster!

WAFFLES

SERVES 6–8

500g plain flour
100g caster sugar
2 teaspoons fast-action yeast
a pinch of salt
100g butter
650ml milk
2 teaspoons vanilla extract
3 eggs
vegetable oil, for greasing

you will need
a waffle iron (I use a sturdy cast-iron one that sits on the hob and which you flip over halfway through cooking)

In a large bowl, stir together the flour, sugar, yeast and salt.

Melt the butter in a saucepan. As soon as it has melted, pour in the milk and vanilla extract and allow it to warm for a couple of minutes. Don't let it get too hot – dip your little finger in; it should feel nicely warm. Pour the liquid over the dry ingredients and whisk together to form a smooth batter.

Separate the eggs, one at a time, into two glasses. After separating each egg, slide the yolk into the batter and the white into a clean mixing bowl. (If you get any yolk in the white they will not whisk up properly, so doing them individually lessens the risk of ruining all three should one yolk split open.) Whisk the yolks into the batter so they are completely amalgamated.

Take a very clean whisk and whisk the egg whites to soft peaks. Using a large metal spoon, fold them gently through the batter mix, trying to keep as much air in as possible. Cover tightly with cling film and leave to prove at room temperature for an hour. You can also prove the batter overnight in the fridge, and then make fresh waffles as a fabulous treat for a weekend breakfast.

Lightly oil the inside of your waffle iron and heat it up as per the manufacturer's instructions. Make sure it's really hot (a little drop of water should sizzle away instantly on contact with the surface), then pour in a ladleful of batter – don't overfill – and shut the lid. Leave to cook, again as per instructions: mine suggests a minute per side. Serve immediately with your favourite toppings.

VARIATIONS
Try one of the following toppings, or mix and match to suit your taste – the options are endless!

- Keep it classic with maple syrup, an old favourite.
- *Dulce de leche* (see page 61) is absolutely delicious spread on a hot waffle.
- All fruit – particularly summer berries, ripe sliced peaches and bananas.
- Melt over a dollop of whipped cream or a scoop of ice cream.
- Add a sprinkle of pecans, walnuts or hazelnuts with syrup or caramel sauce.
- Drizzle over some Nutella – king of the chocolate spreads.
- Add a dollop of fresh fruit compote or jam.

Made from chickpea flour, *socca* is a naturally gluten-free pancake from Nice, in southern France. Here it is wrapped around a classic Niçoise salad – a perfect combination from the shores of the French Riviera. Best eaten in the sunshine with a glass of chilled rosé!

SOCCA NIÇOISE WRAPS

MAKES 6 WRAPS

3 eggs
150g fine green beans, topped, tailed and chopped into 3cm pieces
160g ripe cherry tomatoes, quartered
1 Romano pepper, diced
⅓ cucumber, diced
4 anchovy fillets, chopped
a handful of pitted black olives (preferably Niçoise or Kalamata), sliced
a few basil leaves, roughly torn
vegetable oil, for frying
1 x 225g jar best-quality tuna (I used albacore fillets), drained and flaked
a handful of lamb's lettuce
salt and freshly ground black pepper

for the socca
250g chickpea flour
3 tablespoons olive oil
a sprig of rosemary, needles picked and chopped

for the dressing
3 tablespoons olive oil
2 tablespoons red wine vinegar
1 garlic clove, peeled
a pinch of caster sugar
½ teaspoon Dijon mustard

Begin by making the socca batter. In a bowl, whisk together the chickpea flour with 500ml cold water, the olive oil and rosemary, seasoning well with salt and pepper. Cover and refrigerate for a couple of hours to allow the batter to settle.

For the dressing, place all the ingredients in a sealed jam jar, seasoning to taste with salt and pepper, and give it a good shake. Or for a super-smooth and perfectly emulsified dressing, place all the ingredients in a jug and pulse with a stick blender until creamy. Set aside.

Put the eggs in a pan of cold water, bring to the boil and cook for 5–6 minutes. Run under cold water until cool enough to handle, then peel and slice each one into quarters. Set aside.

Plunge the green beans into boiling water and cook for about 4 minutes until just tender. Drain well and refresh under cold running water to cool quickly and halt cooking. Tip into a large bowl and add the tomatoes, pepper, cucumber, anchovies, olives and basil. Pour over the dressing and stir well to mix. If you are making ahead of time, however, don't dress the salad until you are ready to eat.

Remove the socca batter from the fridge and give it a final whisk to mix. At this point you can divide it between 6 glasses if you like, to make sure the pancakes are of even size. Or you can do as I do and make an educated guess! A ladleful per pancake is about right. Take a large (28–30cm) non-stick frying pan and set it over a medium heat. When it's hot, add a little oil and brush it all over the surface of the pan using a piece of scrunched-up kitchen paper. Make the first pancake by pouring in the batter and swirling it around to spread it out into a round pancake. Let it cook for a couple of minutes then flip over with a fish slice and cook on the other side for a further couple of minutes. Remove to a plate and keep warm in a low oven (around 110°C/90°C Fan/Gas Mark ¼) while you repeat with the rest of the batter to give you 6 pancakes.

To serve, place the pancakes on a plate in the middle of the table, along with the salad, the tuna, the egg quarters and the lettuce, and let your guests fill and wrap their own. Or you can assemble them yourself and wrap tightly in foil ready to eat.

Panisses are deep-fried chickpea flour chips, perfect for dunking in tapenade as a Provençal alternative to fries and ketchup. Begin making the *panisses* in plenty of time, as the batter needs to chill and set before it's sliced and fried.

Note: you will need to begin this recipe at least 6 hours before you want to eat, or even the day before, to allow time for the *panisses* to chill.

PANISSES WITH BLACK OLIVE TAPENADE

MAKES 20 PANISSES, SERVING 4–6 AS A SNACK

25g butter
250g chickpea flour
salt and freshly ground black
   pepper

for the tapenade
150g pitted black olives
   (preferably Niçoise or
   Kalamata)
3 tablespoons capers
3 salted anchovy fillets, rinsed
1 tablespoon finely chopped
   flat-leaf parsley
3 tablespoons olive oil
1 teaspoon red wine vinegar
a grind of black pepper

you will need
a 20cm-square shallow baking
   tin, lined with cling film,
   pressed well into the corners

Place 1 litre of water and the butter in a saucepan and set over a medium heat. Bring to a simmer, allowing the butter to melt, then quickly sieve in the chickpea flour. Use a whisk to beat vigorously for a couple of minutes as the mixture thickens. Reduce the heat to low, season to taste and allow to cook for 10 minutes, stirring regularly. Scrape into the prepared tin, levelling with a spatula (the mixture should be about 1cm thick), and set aside to cool. Once cool, put the tin in the fridge to chill for at least 6 hours or overnight.

For the tapenade, simply place all the ingredients in a food processor and pulse to a paste. Taste and add a little more red wine vinegar or black pepper, if desired. Scoop into a bowl and cover with cling film, leaving at room temperature for an hour or two for the flavours to develop; it will keep in the fridge for up to 3 days.

To cook the *panisses*, turn out the now solid block on to a chopping board and, using a sharp knife, cut into fingers of about 10 x 2cm. Heat the oil in a deep fat fryer to 180°C/350°F and fry in batches for around 5 minutes until deep golden brown and crisp. Drain in a bowl lined with kitchen paper and repeat until they are all cooked.

Serve immediately in a bowl or basket, or tip into a paper cone for the full street experience, with the tapenade dolloped alongside for dipping.

FEUILLAGES ROMANS

ement de glace octogonal entièrement recouvert d'étain repous

La crêpe is one of the most famous dishes in France. If you travel throughout the country you'll see restaurants dedicated to the crêpe, and Paul Bocuse himself has served the famous Crêpe Suzette in his resaurant for 50 years. It also makes for great street food, and this is my version of a crêpe like a banoffee – enjoy!

CRÊPES 'BANOFFEE'

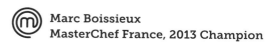

Marc Boissieux
MasterChef France, 2013 Champion

MAKES 8 CRÊPES

3 bananas
50g butter
50ml rum
vanilla ice cream or cream, to
    serve

for the batter
4 eggs, plus 2 egg yolks
250g flour
1 teaspoon caster sugar
pinch of salt
500ml milk
100g butter, melted

for the toffee sauce
50g salted butter
100g caster sugar
150ml double cream

To make the batter, combine the eggs, yolks, flour, sugar and salt in a large bowl and mix for a few minutes. Add the milk gradually and whisk until the batter is homogeneous. Continue to whisk as you add the melted butter. Leave the batter to rest in the fridge for an hour.

While the batter is resting, make the sauce. Cut the butter into small cubes. Place half the sugar in a pan and heat slowly. Place the cream in another pan and heat slowly.

When the sugar becomes liquid caramel, add the remaining sugar. When it is brown in colour, remove from the heat and add the butter, whisking slowly. Add the hot cream, mix together and set aside to cool.

Cut the bananas into discs. Put half the butter in a pan to heat. Add the bananas and cook for a minute. Add the rum and blaze for seconds before removing from the heat.

For the crêpes, melt a little of the remaining butter in a frying pan, add a ladleful of batter and swirl to coat the base of the pan. Cook for 1–2 minutes, then flip over and cook for a further minute. Scatter a few banana discs on to each crêpe and sprinkle with the toffee sauce. Fold in half then half again to form a triangle. Repeat until all the batter is used. Serve with vanilla ice cream or whipped cream.

From the mountainous southern region of Germany, *flamkuchen* are thin, crisp pizzas topped with a dreamy combination of melting onions, cream, cheese and smoked bacon. I can't think of a more perfect accompaniment to an ice-cold beer or two.

FLAMKUCHEN

MAKES 4 FLAMKUCHEN

450g strong bread flour
½ teaspoon salt
½ teaspoon fast-action yeast
3 tablespoons olive oil, plus
    extra for greasing
300ml hand-hot water
40g butter
700g onions, thinly sliced
8 tablespoons crème fraîche
200g smoked lardons
200g Gruyère cheese, grated
salt, freshly ground black pepper
    and freshly grated nutmeg
snipped chives, to garnish

Make the pizza base in a food mixer or by hand. Stir together the flour, salt and yeast until mixed, then add 2 tablespoons of olive oil and the water, kneading together until smooth and elastic. This will take around 10 minutes by hand; around 5 minutes in a food mixer with a dough hook. Scrape the dough into a clean, lightly oiled bowl and cover loosely with a clean tea towel. Leave to prove while you cook the onions.

Melt the butter and the remaining tablespoon of oil in a deep saucepan and add the sliced onions. Cook over a really low heat, stirring every now and then, until the onions are soft but not coloured. This will take around 40–45 minutes, maybe even a touch longer; don't try to rush the process – slow-cooked onions take on an incredible depth of flavour and in this simple dish that is the key to success. A deep saucepan helps prevent the onions from burning as they cook in a thick, dense layer.

Preheat the oven to 240°C/220°C Fan/Gas Mark 9. Divide the dough into 4 even pieces, and stretch and roll each to a thin disc of about 22–24cm in diameter. Lay each on a baking tray (if you don't have 4 suitable trays, lay them on separate sheets of baking parchment ready to slide on to trays to bake in shifts). Top each base with a couple of tablespoons of crème fraîche and season all over with salt, pepper and a generous grind of fresh nutmeg. Dot spoonfuls of the cooked onions over each base and scatter on the lardons. Finally sprinkle over the grated Gruyère cheese and bake in the hot oven, in batches if necessary, until the base is crisp and the cheese golden and bubbling, about 12–14 minutes.

Garnish with the snipped chives and ideally serve straight from the oven, although this still tastes great at room temperature or even cold.

Funnily enough, *leberkäse* translates literally from the German as 'liver cheese', despite there being neither liver nor cheese in this meatloaf recipe. Hugely popular in the Bavarian region, it is often served sliced, fried and piled into a burger with mayo, gherkins, mustard and crisp onions, as I have done here. The texture of the meat is really fine, much like a hot dog, and it tastes like a spicy sausage. The curing salt is not essential, but it does keep the meat nicely pink; substituting ordinary salt is fine but the loaf will be darker in colour.

LEBERKÄSE

SERVES 6–8

2 teaspoons white pepper, preferably freshly ground
1 teaspoon curing salt
1 teaspoon mace or nutmeg
1 teaspoon coriander seeds, preferably freshly ground
1 tablespoon marjoram leaves, chopped
3 onions: 1 roughly chopped, 2 thinly sliced
2 garlic cloves, chopped
180g rindless smoked bacon, chopped
500g minced beef
500g minced pork
350ml ice-cold water
2 tablespoons olive oil
6–8 crusty bread rolls, warmed and sliced open
a handful of lettuce, chopped
4–6 gherkins, sliced lengthways
mustard, to taste (ideally German, or use your favourite)
vegetable oil, for greasing

for the chive mayonnaise
6 tablespoons mayonnaise
a small bunch of chives, snipped
freshly ground black pepper

you will need
a 21 x 12cm loaf tin, brushed inside with vegetable oil

Preheat the oven to 180°C/160°C Fan/Gas Mark 4.

Place the pepper, salt, mace or nutmeg, coriander, marjoram, chopped onion and garlic in a food processor and whizz to a pulp. Add the bacon and process again until well blended and quite smooth. With the motor running, drop spoonfuls of mince into the processor, allowing it to process for about 20 seconds or so before adding more. Once both the beef and pork mince have been added, keeping the motor running, pour in the ice-cold water in a steady trickle. Allow everything to process for another couple of minutes until you have a really smooth pâté-like paste. If your processor bowl is on the small side you may need to do this in a couple of batches to get it smooth enough, then beat the batches together to a uniform emulsion.

Scrape the mixture into the prepared loaf tin, pressing it well into the corners and mounding it up and smoothing the surface so it looks like a raised loaf of bread. Don't worry that the tin is full to overflowing – it won't rise as it cooks and by mounding it high you will get nice big slices when you cut it. Wet a sharp knife with cold water. Make diagonal slashes across the surface to form a diamond pattern, wiping and re-wetting the knife as you go so it doesn't stick. Put the tin on to a baking tray and slide into the oven. Bake for about an hour and 15 minutes, until it's browned on the surface and has pulled away from the sides of the tin. It should be piping hot all the way through – if you have a meat thermometer, it should read 75°C/170°F in the centre; if you don't, insert a skewer into the centre and leave it for 20 seconds, then touch it quickly to your bottom lip – it should feel hot rather than lukewarm.

While the meatloaf is cooking, make the chive mayonnaise by stirring the mayonnaise and chives together in a small bowl and seasoning with a little pepper. Set aside.

Place the oil and sliced onions in a large frying pan and set over a medium heat, frying until starting to soften and lightly golden, about 10 minutes. Turn off the heat and set aside until the meatloaf is cooked.

Once the meatloaf is out of the oven, remove it from the tin and place on to a chopping board. It should come out easily, skewered on to a fork at each end. Cut into 2cm-thick slices.

Set the onions back over a medium heat, pushing them to one side of the pan. Fry the slices of *leberkäse* for a minute or so on each side until crisp. You may need to do this in batches, depending on the size of your pan. The onions should caramelise nicely alongside the slices of meatloaf – if they are getting too browned, lift them out on to a plate.

To assemble the rolls, spread the chive mayonnaise on the base of each, and top with a little lettuce and a few slices of gherkin. Add a slice of *leberkäse* to each, followed by a few onions. Spread a little mustard on to the top half of the bun and press it down on to the burger. Serve immediately.

A staple snack at Christmas markets across Germany, *kartoffelpuffer* are crisp potato pancakes served with a dollop of tart apple sauce. These make a great snack with a glass of cold beer, or try them with a warming *glühwein*, just as they would in Germany.

KARTOFFELPUFFER

MAKES ABOUT 20 KARTOFFELPUFFER, SERVING AROUND 6 AS A SNACK

1kg floury potatoes
1 large onion
3 tablespoons plain flour
2 eggs
1–2 teaspoons horseradish
   sauce or mustard (optional)
vegetable oil, for frying
salt and freshly ground black
   pepper

for the apple sauce
2 Bramley apples
1 tablespoon granulated sugar,
   or to taste

Peel the potatoes and grate them into a bowl. Grate in the onion and add the flour and eggs, stirring well to mix together. Season generously with salt and pepper and stir in the horseradish or mustard, if using. Set aside.

For the apple sauce, peel, core and chop the apples, dropping them into a saucepan as you go. Add 2 tablespoons of water and set over a medium heat, covering with a lid. Allow to cook until soft, about 5–8 minutes, mashing them with a spoon from time to time to help them along. Season to taste with a little sugar, bearing in mind that the sauce is supposed to be quite tart, and spoon into a bowl to cool a little. The sauce can be served warm or made in advance and served cold.

Add 2–3 tablespoons of vegetable oil to a large frying pan and set over a high heat. Once the oil is hot, dollop a few tablespoons of the potato mixture into the pan, flattening them out until around 1cm thick, and allow to fry for 2–3 minutes until crisp and golden. Flip over with a palette knife and fry on the other side. Remove to a plate lined with kitchen paper and keep warm in a low oven (around 110°C/90°C Fan/Gas Mark ¼) while you make the rest.

Serve hot with a dollop of apple sauce on top.

Biksemad is a traditional Danish dish created from leftovers of meat and boiled potatoes – typically meat from a beef or pork roast – and served with fried eggs, pickled vegetables and condiments such as ketchup, HP sauce and Worcestershire sauce. Traditionally, the dish is made by cutting meat and potatoes into bite-sized cubes and frying them with onions before serving, but I prefer to cook the ingredients individually and combine them afterwards.

BIKSEMAD

 Anders Halskov-Jensen
MasterChef Denmark, 2015 Champion

SERVES ABOUT 4

2 tablespoons olive oil
600g boiled and cooled potatoes, cut into 2–3cm cubes
50g butter
200g onions, thinly sliced
400g cold roast pork or beef, cut into 2–3cm cubes
sprigs of fresh thyme
1 egg per person
salt and freshly ground black pepper

Place the oil in a frying pan over a high heat and fry the potato cubes until they have a nice golden crust. Season with salt and pepper and set aside.

Place half the butter in the frying pan and fry the onions at medium heat until they soften and start to brown a little. The idea is to bring out the sweetness in the onions without frying too much. Set aside.

Fry the meat cubes gently in the remaining butter. Since the meat is already cooked, it should just be warmed through. Add the potatoes and the onions, mix everything together and season with thyme leaves and salt and pepper, to taste.

Serve the *biksemad* with 1 fried egg per person, alongside condiments and pickled vegetables such as beetroots and gherkins. If you can get it, Danish rye bread with butter is a nice side dish.

VARIATIONS
You can upgrade the *biksemad* by adding:

- Cubes of fried bacon.
- Slices of fried sausage.
- Homemade béarnaise sauce (in my family this version is known as *Dronningebiks* [The Queen's *biksemad*]).

Ubiquitous across Finland, often eaten as a snack with a glass of cold milk, these buns are translated literally as 'slapped ears' – some say because of their slightly squished shape, and others because children who tried to steal them hot from the oven were told they would get their ears slapped.

Note: you will need to begin this recipe several hours before you want to eat, or even the day before, to allow time for the dough to prove.

KORVAPUUSTI

MAKES ABOUT 26 KORVAPUUSTI

150g butter, softened
80g caster sugar
1 tablespoon ground cinnamon
1 egg, lightly beaten
2–3 tablespoons pearl sugar, or granulated sugar (if you can't find pearl sugar)

for the dough

1 heaped tablespoon cardamom pods, or 1 tablespoon ground cardamom
950g strong white bread flour
200g caster sugar
2 teaspoons fast-action yeast
1 teaspoon salt
500ml lukewarm milk
2 eggs
150g butter, softened, plus extra for greasing

Start by making the dough. If using whole cardamom pods, bruise them with the flat of a large knife, peel and discard the skins, and place the seeds into a spice mill or pestle and mortar. Grind to a powder then tip into a food mixer or large bowl. If using ground cardamom, simply place it straight into the food mixer or bowl.

Add the flour, sugar, yeast and salt and, using the dough hook of the mixer, or with a wooden spoon if you are making by hand, mix together thoroughly. I would not advise attempting the next stage by hand as the dough is very wet, so place all the dry ingredients in the bowl of a food mixer and add the milk, eggs and butter. Mix on a low speed until combined. Turn the motor up to medium and knead for 5 minutes until smooth and elastic.

Lightly grease a large, clean bowl with a little soft butter and scrape the dough into it. Cover and leave to prove until doubled in size – about 3 hours at room temperature or overnight in the fridge; I prefer a slow overnight prove so they are ready for breakfast the following day.

For the filling, beat the butter, sugar and cinnamon together in a bowl to form a smooth, soft paste. Set aside.

Tip the dough on to a lightly floured worktop and cut it in half. Roll each piece out to a large rectangle, approximately 50 x 30cm in size and 5mm thick. Spread the spiced butter thinly and evenly over the 2 sheets of dough, then roll each up snugly to form a long sausage shape. Cut each length into triangles by slicing through on the diagonal, first one way, then the opposite (you should get about 26). You want the tip of the triangle to be about 2cm wide, and the base to be about 6–7cm. Then, with a triangle in front of you, base side closest, press your finger firmly down the centre from the tip to the base. This will flatten the top and squish out each end to reveal the spirals of spiced butter. Repeat with the other triangles. Arrange them, well spaced out, on 2 or 3 baking trays and leave to prove once more for 30 minutes.

Preheat the oven to 220°C/200°C Fan/Gas Mark 7. Just before you bake, brush the surface of each bun with a little beaten egg and sprinkle on some pearl sugar (or granulated sugar). You can freeze them at this stage: leave on the baking trays to freeze, then pack into a bag or tub and leave in the freezer until ready to cook.

Bake in the hot oven for about 15 minutes, until deep golden brown. If cooking from frozen, give them an extra couple of minutes. Serve warm.

These traditional Polish dumplings are fairly easy but pretty time-consuming to make. For me, their rich woodland flavours make them the perfect street food for making on a wild, wet autumn afternoon – they really are comfort food *extraordinaire*.

PIEROGI

MAKES ABOUT 42 PIEROGI, SERVING ABOUT 6

75g unsalted butter, plus extra for frying
3 tablespoons olive oil
4 onions: 2 finely chopped, 2 thinly sliced
1 large potato (about 400g), peeled and grated
250g white mushrooms, finely chopped
1 teaspoon caraway seeds, coarsely ground
8 rashers smoked streaky bacon
4–6 tablespoons soured cream
a small bunch of chives, snipped
salt and freshly ground black pepper

for the dough
500g plain flour, plus extra for rolling
½ teaspoon salt
2 tablespoons soured cream or full-fat yogurt
olive oil, for kneading

To make the dough, stir the flour and salt together in a large bowl. Pour in 200ml water and add the soured cream or yogurt, stirring to bring it together into a flaky ball. Tip on to a lightly oiled worktop and knead for 5 minutes until smooth and shiny. Wrap in cling film and chill in the fridge for an hour or so (up to 24 hours is fine).

Meanwhile, melt 25g butter and 1 tablespoon olive oil together in a large frying pan set over a medium-low heat. Add the chopped onion and allow to soften and lightly caramelise for 10–15 minutes. Stir through the grated potato, mushrooms and caraway seeds and season well with salt and pepper.

Tear off a sheet of baking parchment and scrunch it up under running water. Shake off the excess water and spread it out over the filling in the frying pan, tucking it snuggly around the edges to create a steamy lid. Reduce the heat to low and cook gently for a further 15 minutes until the potato is soft and collapsing, stirring occasionally to incorporate the caramelised bits on the base of the pan. Turn off the heat, scoop this filling mixture into a dish and leave to cool.

Wipe out the frying pan and set back over a medium heat. Add the remaining oil and fry the bacon until crisp on both sides. Set aside to drain briefly on a plate lined with a couple of sheets of kitchen paper, then snip into pieces. Add the sliced onions and remaining 50g butter to the pan and gently fry until soft and lightly caramelised, about 20 minutes. Scoop into another dish and set aside. Give the frying pan a wipe clean.

Take the ball of chilled dough from the fridge and roll it out on a lightly floured worktop until it's about 2mm thick. Take a 10cm cutter and stamp out as many circles as you can, then re-roll the scraps and cut a few more circles until you have used as much of the dough as possible.

To fill the *pierogi*, take one circle and place a heaped teaspoon of filling on one side, leaving a border around the edge. Dampen the border with a little cold water using a clean finger or small brush. Fold the other half of the circle over the filling, pressing the edges together to seal the filling inside, then crimp and roll the edges over so they look like miniature pasties. Set aside on a well-floured baking tray. Repeat until you have used up all the circles and filling.

When you are ready to cook, bring a large pan of lightly salted water to the boil over a high heat. Add about a third of the *pierogi* and simmer rapidly until they all bob to the surface, about 4–5 minutes. Scoop out with a slotted spoon, allowing the water to drain back into the pan, and tip them on to a lightly oiled baking tray. Cook the remaining *pierogi* in 2 more batches, placing them on to the baking tray in a single layer when done – use 2 sheets if necessary so they don't stick together.

Add a little butter to the cleaned frying pan and let it melt over a medium heat. Fry the *pierogi* in batches for a minute or so on each side until crisp. Then transfer to a dish and keep warm in a low oven (around 110°C/90°C Fan/Gas Mark ¼).

Once all the *pierogi* are fried, tip the onions back into the pan to warm through, along with the bacon.

To serve, divide the *pierogi* between plates, spoon over a few onions and bits of bacon, drizzle on a little soured cream and scatter with a few chives.

Nicknamed the 'Polish pizza', and hugely popular on the streets across Poland, *zapiekanki* are open toasted sandwiches topped with sautéed mushrooms and melted cheese. Said to hail from the Communist days of the 1970s when food was scarce, this is a cheap and deliciously comforting snack. You could embellish it with other vegetables, such as roasted peppers or sweetcorn, but I prefer the simplicity of the earthy mushrooms and oozing cheese. The ketchup is absolutely *de rigueur*, so even if you think you don't like it I urge you to give it a go.

ZAPIEKANKI

SERVES 2

25g butter
1 tablespoon olive oil
500g white mushrooms, sliced
1 garlic clove, crushed (optional)
20–25cm piece of long, thin baguette
100–140g grated hard cheese, such as mature Cheddar, smoked Cheddar or Gouda
salt and freshly ground black pepper
a few chives, snipped, to garnish
ketchup

Melt the butter and oil together in a frying pan and throw in the mushrooms and the garlic, if using. Season with salt and pepper and sauté over a medium heat for about 10 minutes, until the mushrooms are soft.

Preheat the oven to 200°C/180°C Fan/Gas Mark 6. Slice the baguette in half lengthways and lay the pieces on a baking tray. If they are a little wobbly, make a support for the wobbly edge with a piece of kitchen foil screwed into a pencil shape. Once the mushrooms are cooked, divide them evenly between the pieces of baguette and top with the cheese.

Bake in the oven for 6–7 minutes until the bread is crisp and the cheese melted. Sprinkle each with a few chives and garnish with a squiggle of ketchup for true authenticity. Eat immediately, napkin at the ready.

Probably Ottoman in origin – and similar to the various *borek* (stuffed pastries) enjoyed by the Turkish – *burek* is quite specifically a Bosnian pastry of homemade filo type, stretched as thin as paper, stuffed with a spiced beef filling and coiled up like a snake. The pastry takes a bit of courage: it will almost certainly be the thinnest dough you ever work with, but the trick is to go slowly when stretching so that it thins out without too many holes appearing.

BUREK

SERVES 4–6

2 tablespoons olive oil, plus
   extra for rolling
500g minced beef
1 large onion, finely chopped
2 garlic cloves, crushed
2 teaspoons paprika
2 teaspoons ground allspice
500ml beef stock
a small bunch of flat-leaf
   parsley, chopped
salt and freshly ground black
   pepper, plus extra sea salt
   flakes for sprinkling
plain yogurt, to serve

for the pastry
450g plain flour
1 teaspoon salt

Add the oil to a deep frying pan set over a high heat. When the oil is hot, tip in the mince, breaking it up with a wooden spoon as it heats. Stir fry for a good 10–15 minutes until it's brown and crisp in places. This caramelisation adds loads of flavour, so I prefer to brown my mince before adding any onion. Reduce the heat to low and add the onion, frying for another 10 minutes to soften slightly. Add the garlic, paprika and allspice and fry briefly – for another minute or two – before pouring in the stock. Season with salt and pepper and bring to the boil. Cook for about 40 minutes, uncovered, stirring from time to time as it reduces. You want a rich mince sauce that's not too wet, otherwise it will make your pastry soggy. Turn off the heat, stir through the parsley, then scoop the filling into a bowl and set aside until completely cold. You can make the filling well ahead of time (up to 3 days) and chill in the fridge.

For the pastry, simply mix the flour and salt together in a bowl and gradually pour in 300ml cold water, stirring to bring it together into a ball. Tip on to a lightly floured worktop and knead for a few minutes until smooth. Cover with cling film and leave to rest for 30 minutes.

Clear your worktop or kitchen table – you will need a big space as the dough will be rolled to a circle of around 55–60cm. Spread a thin layer of oil on the surface and over a rolling pin and begin to roll out the dough, turning it regularly to keep the shape as circular as possible. Use plenty of oil to make sure it doesn't stick. Once it's as thin as you can roll it, switch to your hands, coating them with a little oil first. You want to slowly and gently stretch the dough as thin as you possibly can: it will become pretty much see-through in places. If little holes or tears appear, push the edges back together.

Preheat the oven to 220°C/200°C Fan/Gas Mark 7. Once you have your large circle of dough, take the cold filling and spread some of it little by little into a large 1cm-thick ring about 3cm from the outer edge of the pastry. When you have a complete circle of meat, fold up the edge of the pastry to enclose the meat. Then continue to roll over so you are wrapping the meat in several layers of pastry, working bit by bit all the way round. Once you have rolled the meat in about three layers of pastry, take a small knife and cut through all the way round so you have a long circular sausage shape. Make a cut through the pastry to break the circle into one long sausage shape, then slide one end carefully on to a baking tray and coil it around and around in a spiral.

Go back to the remaining pastry, which will now be a smaller circle, and repeat the process once more. Trim away the centre of the circle and discard, then coil this sausage around the other on the baking tray. Sprinkle over a few flakes of sea salt and slide into the hot oven. Bake for about 45–50 minutes until golden brown and crisp.

Serve hot or at room temperature, cut into wedges, with a traditional dollop of plain yogurt.

This super-easy fried cheese snack from the Czech Republic ticks all the street food satisfaction boxes – crisp outside, oozing melting middle, and a sharp, tangy sauce to go with it. The trick to getting a crunchy exterior with the cheese melting all over the pan is the double coating of egg and breadcrumbs, so don't scrimp on this step.

SMAŽENÝ SÝR WITH TARTARE SAUCE

SERVES 4 AS A SNACK

2 tablespoons plain flour
2 eggs, lightly beaten with a
  little salt and pepper
170g fresh breadcrumbs
460g Edam or Gouda cheese,
  cut into 4 thick wedges
vegetable oil, for frying
chopped chives, to garnish

for the tartare sauce
4 tablespoons mayonnaise
1 tablespoon cider vinegar
2 teaspoons mustard
½ small onion, finely grated
3 or 4 gherkins, finely chopped
finely grated zest of ½ lemon
salt and freshly ground black
  pepper

Place the flour in a shallow bowl, the eggs in another and the breadcrumbs in a third. Take a wedge of cheese and roll it in the flour, then dip into the egg, submerging it to wet it all over. Then roll in the breadcrumbs until completely coated. Set aside on a plate and repeat with the other 3 pieces of cheese. Then re-dip each one into the remaining egg, and roll once more in the breadcrumbs to give each piece a second coat. Return to the plate and chill in the fridge for an hour.

Meanwhile, make the tartare sauce by mixing together the mayonnaise, vinegar, mustard, onion, gherkins and lemon zest in a small bowl. Season to taste with salt and pepper and set aside.

Take a large frying pan, pour in a good 5mm of oil and set over a medium-high heat. Once the oil is hot, fry the cheese wedges for 2–3 minutes on each side until bronzed and crisp.

Serve immediately while the cheese is still molten, garnished with the chives, and with the tartare sauce dolloped alongside to dunk in as you eat.

These lemony Greek kebabs are best made with a succulent, not-too-lean cut of pork, such as leg or shoulder, as the marbling of fat through the meat bastes the kebabs from the inside as they cook. You could use low-fat tenderloin if you prefer, but the result will be a touch drier.

Note: you will need to begin this recipe several hours before you want to eat, or even the day before, as the pork needs time to marinate.

SOUVLAKI PITTAS WITH TZATZIKI

MAKES 6 LARGE PITTAS

800g pork, cut into 3cm cubes
2 tablespoons olive oil
2 garlic cloves, crushed
juice and finely grated zest of 1 lemon
1 teaspoon dried oregano
a pinch of dried chilli flakes
6 large pitta breads
3 large tomatoes, sliced
1 small red onion, thinly sliced
freshly ground black pepper
lemon wedges, to serve

for the tzatziki
½ large cucumber
1 teaspoon fine salt
300g full-fat Greek yogurt
2 garlic cloves
a small bunch of mint, leaves finely chopped

you will need
6 metal or bamboo skewers (if using bamboo, soak in cold water for an hour before using to prevent them from burning)

Place the pork in a large bowl with the oil, garlic, lemon juice and zest, oregano, chilli flakes and a generous grind of black pepper. Mix together thoroughly and leave to marinate for at least 2 hours, or ideally overnight in the fridge.

Make the tzatziki by grating the cucumber, skin and all, into a sieve hung over a bowl. Sprinkle over the salt, stirring well to mix, and leave for 30 minutes. Squeeze out any excess liquid and add the cucumber to a small bowl along with the yogurt, garlic and mint. Stir to mix and set aside.

When you are ready to eat, fire up a barbecue or set a griddle pan over a high heat until it's smoking hot. Thread the pork evenly between 6 skewers and cook over a high heat for 10–12 minutes, turning regularly, until the kebabs are golden and lightly charred in places.

Lightly toast the pitta breads and split open. Fill each with the meat from a kebab and a generous dollop of tzatziki; finish with a little tomato and onion, and lemon wedges alongside to squeeze over.

These feta and filo pies are sold in bakeries throughout Greece, where they are usually bought as a late breakfast or mid-morning snack and eaten on the run. I think *tiropita* taste best warm rather than piping hot from the oven, so they make a fantastic on-the-go street food.

TIROPITA

MAKES 1 LARGE PIE, SERVING ABOUT 6

200g feta, crumbled
150g full-fat Greek yogurt
75g Parmesan cheese, finely grated
3 eggs
¼ freshly grated nutmeg
12 sheets filo pastry (a 220g pack)
75g butter, melted
1 tablespoon sesame seeds
freshly ground black pepper

you will need
a 22cm square baking tin lined with a strip of baking parchment (for ease of lifting from the tin)

Preheat the oven to 200°C/180°C Fan/Gas Mark 6.

In a large bowl, mix together the feta, yogurt, Parmesan and eggs. Add a generous grating of nutmeg and season well with black pepper. Set aside.

Take out 6 sheets of filo from the pack, keeping the rest well wrapped up so they don't get dry and cracked. Working quickly, lightly brush melted butter over each sheet, using them to line the base and sides of the tin. Depending on the size of the sheets and the shape of the tin, you may need to overlap the sheets to ensure that the base and sides are fully covered.

Pour the filling into the tin, levelling it with the back of a spoon. Then brush the remaining pastry sheets with butter and lay each over the filling, again overlapping as necessary to ensure the filling is completely encased in pastry. Finish by brushing the last of the butter on the top and sprinkling over the sesame seeds.

Bake in the oven for about 30 minutes until the pastry is golden and the filling set; a gentle prod will help you decide – it should feel firm to the touch. Allow to cool a little before lifting from the tin to cut and serve.

Arancini, derived from the Italian for 'little orange', are crisp fried balls of creamy risotto from Sicily. Traditionally stuffed with a little ragù, in this recipe they are filled with roast squash and gorgonzola. Making *arancini* is a bit of a fiddly, messy business, but worth it for such a delicious combination of crunchy exterior and creamy cheesy squidge inside. My best advice is to start the rolling and coating process with a clear and organised worktop, and to stop when your hands are a total mess – wash and dry them, then continue!

ARANCINI WITH ROAST SQUASH AND GORGONZOLA

MAKES 12 ARANCINI, SERVING ABOUT 6

a pinch of saffron threads
450g butternut squash, cut into 2cm cubes
3 tablespoons olive oil
50g butter
1 large onion, finely chopped
2 garlic cloves, crushed
350g carnaroli risotto rice
250ml white wine, or more stock (see below) if you prefer
750ml chicken or vegetable stock
90g freshly grated Parmesan
60g gorgonzola, cut into twelve 1cm cubes
100g plain flour
2 eggs, lightly beaten
120g panko breadcrumbs
salt and freshly ground black pepper

Preheat the oven to 200°C/180°C Fan/Gas Mark 6. Soak the saffron threads in 1 tablespoon of boiling water.

Place the butternut squash in a roasting tin with 2 tablespoons olive oil, season lightly and cook for 20–25 minutes, until soft.

Place the remaining oil and half the butter in a heavy-based pan and set over a medium heat. As the butter melts, tip in the onion, reduce the heat to as low as possible and allow to cook gently for about 20 minutes, until soft but not coloured.

Increase the heat to medium, stir through the garlic and fry for just a minute before adding in the rice. Stir fry for a couple of minutes until the grains start to turn translucent, then pour in the wine, if using, or extra stock. Stir frequently over a medium heat until the liquid is almost absorbed, then pour in about a third of the stock, along with the saffron water, and keep cooking and stirring for around 5–8 minutes until the liquid is almost absorbed. Add another third of the stock and repeat, then add the remaining stock, stirring regularly until it has absorbed and the rice is just tender. Turn off the heat and stir through the rest of the butter and the Parmesan. Season to taste with salt and pepper and set aside to cool – spreading it out on a tray will speed this up considerably.

Roughly mash the roasted squash on a chopping board, then divide it into 12 equal portions. Flatten each portion out to a disc, then place a cube of gorgonzola in the centre, before covering it over by drawing up the squash around the sides.

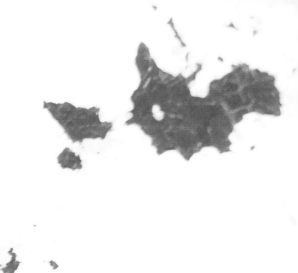

Place the flour, egg and breadcrumbs in separate bowls.

Clear the worktop and set up a production line: the risotto, followed by the squash filling, the bowl of flour, bowl of egg, bowl of breadcrumbs and finally a clean plate to put the finished *arancini* on.

Take a generous tablespoon of risotto, or alternatively weigh the cooked risotto and divide it by 12 to give you equal portions: it's extra work, but worth it. Roll the first piece of risotto into a ball in your palms, pressing it firmly together. Then flatten the ball out and add a ball of squash filling to the middle, drawing up the sides of the risotto to completely enclose it as a sphere. Drop the ball into the bowl of flour and roll it gently until coated all over. Then transfer it to the bowl of egg, rolling again until coated, before finally dropping and rolling it in the bowl of breadcrumbs. Set aside on the clean plate and repeat for the other 11 *arancini*.

Heat the oil in a deep fat fryer to 170°C/340°F. Fry the *arancini* in batches of 3 or 4 for about 5 minutes, until crisp and golden.

VARIATIONS
Feel free to experiment with different fillings. You could try:

- Leftover bolognese sauce.
- A mixture of ham and mozzarella.
- Capers and sundried tomatoes.

Polpette are little flavoursome Italian meatballs, normally served as a snack or appetiser rather than with the perhaps more familiar bowl of spaghetti. The trick to a soft and tender meatball is to soak the breadcrumbs in milk before you add the rest of the ingredients.

Note: you may wish to begin this recipe the day before you want to eat, to allow the flavours to develop.

POLPETTE

MAKES ABOUT 35 BITE-SIZED MEATBALLS, SERVING 6–8 AS A SNACK

100g fresh breadcrumbs
150ml milk
500g minced pork or veal, or a mixture of both
50g freshly grated Parmesan
1 egg
finely grated zest of 1 lemon
1 garlic clove, crushed
a small bunch of flat-leaf parsley, chopped
2 tablespoons olive oil, for frying
salt and freshly ground black pepper

for the tomato sauce
1 large red onion, finely chopped
4 tablespoons olive oil
3 garlic cloves, crushed
2 x 400g cans chopped plum tomatoes
2 teaspoons granulated sugar, to taste

Place the breadcrumbs in a large bowl and pour over the milk. Leave to soak until the milk is completely absorbed, about 10 minutes. Add the mince, Parmesan, egg, lemon zest, garlic, parsley and a generous seasoning of salt and pepper. Mix together with your hands until thoroughly combined. Wash your hands and shake dry. Using damp hands, roll the mixture into little walnut-sized balls and lay on a baking tray; you should get about 35. At this point you can cover with cling film and leave to rest in the fridge for up to 24 hours; this isn't essential but it does allow plenty of time for the flavours to develop.

To make the sauce, add the onion and half the olive oil to a saucepan and set over a medium-low heat. Fry the onion for 15 minutes until starting to soften, then stir through the garlic and fry for a further minute. Pour in the tomatoes, add the sugar and season to taste with salt and pepper. Simmer steadily, stirring from time to time, until the sauce is rich and thick, about 25–30 minutes. Stir through the remaining olive oil.

While the sauce is simmering, cook the meatballs. Take your largest frying pan, add the olive oil and set over a medium-high heat. Once the oil is hot, add the meatballs in a single layer. They need to have a little space around them so you can turn them easily, and you may need to cook them in 2 batches. The meatballs need about 20 minutes of gentle frying, so they're cooked through to the centre and develop a lovely golden crust all over. Turn them regularly – I'm more dextrous with 2 forks, but use tongs if you prefer – but don't turn them too soon or they'll stick to the pan; allow a golden crust to form before attempting it.

To serve, spoon a puddle of sauce into a dish and top with the meatballs.

This is a delightfully moreish but wonderfully simple recipe from the deep south of Italy. These deep-fried courgette and aubergine sticks are best eaten as soon as you make them, but be warned: they will be really hot so nibble gingerly at first.

VERDURI FRITTI

SERVES 4–6

2 large or 3 medium courgettes (about 450g)
2 aubergines (about 600g)
150g self-raising flour
75g Parmesan, finely grated
100ml milk
salt and freshly ground black pepper

Slice the courgettes and aubergines into sticks about the size of your index finger.

Heat the oil in a deep fat fryer to 180°C/350°F.

Place the flour and Parmesan in a shallow bowl, season well with salt and pepper and stir until combined. Add the milk to another shallow bowl, and have a large baking tray handy.

Take a small handful of the vegetable sticks and roll them in the flour mixture. Shake off the excess and dip briefly in the milk, before dipping back into the flour mixture to coat all over. Spread out on the baking tray and repeat with the rest of the vegetables.

Fry in the hot oil in batches for about 2–3 minutes until crisp and golden. Drain on kitchen paper and eat immediately.

There are a few things I like to the eat the most when I go back to Italy: *gnocco fritto* is definitely one of them. I crave it so much when I am here in the States that it becomes a special treat when I am back home. Fluffy, crunchy and so flavourful, *gnocco fritto* is ideal with every little snack or even instead of bread at dinner time. It's literally fried bread! I use it a lot like a sandwich: a combination of stracchino and mortadella is for sure my favorite filling, but don't give any limits to your fantasy because you can dress a *gnocco fritto* in anyway you prefer. I am sure that with this easy recipe *gnocco fritto* will soon become one of your favourites as well! *Buon appetito!*

GNOCCO FRITTO

 Luca Manfè
MasterChef USA, 2013 Champion

MAKES 12–15 GNOCCO

12g fresh yeast
1 teaspoon caster sugar
175ml warm water
500g plain flour
70g butter or lard
10g salt
vegetable oil, for deep frying
400g stracchino (use taleggio
    or mozzarella if you can't find
    stracchino)
200g mortadella

Crumble the fresh yeast into a bowl, add the sugar, then pour over 50ml warm water and let the yeast melt, stirring with a spoon. Add 2 tablespoons of flour to form a very soft batter and leave it to rest for half an hour.

After 30 minutes, place the remaining flour into a large bowl and add the batter and the butter or lard. Dissolve the salt in the remaining warm water, then pour all the water into the bowl and begin to knead the dough.

When the liquid has been fully incorporated into the flour, transfer the dough to a floured surface and knead until it becomes smooth and homogeneous. Bring the dough into a ball shape and cut a cross into the top of the ball.

Place the dough in a large bowl that has been sprinkled with a handful of flour and cover the bowl with cling film. Leave to rise for about 4 hours in a warm and dry environment, until the dough has approximately tripled in volume. When the dough is ready, knead it on a floured surface and roll it out to a sheet about 3mm thin and cut it into 8–10cm diamonds or squares.

Half fill a pan with vegetable oil and heat it to 180°C/350°F. Dip a few *gnocco* at a time into the oil and fry for 4–5 minutes until golden brown. Turn over halfway through. Remove them with a slotted spoon and place on a piece of kitchen paper to remove the excess oil.

While still warm, cut each one in half and put 1 or 2 thin slices of stracchino in the middle with a couple of pieces of mortadella and eat it like a *panino*!

It is imperative to serve this with a glass of red wine – *buon appetito*, beautiful people!

The Spanish answer to a pasty, these little pastries are stuffed full of tuna amd sweet onions and peppers, and are heady with the scent of smoked paprika. For the very best flavour, they are great served warm, rather than hot, making them the ideal candidate for a street-food picnic.

EMPANADILLAS DE ATUN

MAKES 12 EMPANADILLAS

4 tablespoons olive oil
3 large onions, sliced
3 large peppers (I use 1 each of
    red, green and yellow), thinly
    sliced
3 garlic cloves, crushed
1 teaspoon smoked paprika
1 tablespoon sherry vinegar
a bunch of flat-leaf parsley,
    chopped
2 x 160g cans tuna, drained
3 hard-boiled eggs, peeled and
    sliced
1 egg, beaten
salt and freshly ground black
    pepper, plus extra sea salt
    flakes for sprinkling

for the dough
350g strong white bread flour
125g fine polenta
1 teaspoon fast-action yeast
½ teaspoon fine salt
100ml white wine
25ml olive oil
50g lard or vegetable fat, cut
    into small cubes
1 egg, beaten
6–8 tablespoons warm water
vegetable oil, for greasing

In a large bowl, by hand or in a food mixer with a dough attachment, mix together the flour, polenta, yeast and salt for the dough. Pour in the wine and olive oil and add the lard or fat and the beaten egg. Add enough warm water to bring it all together into a soft, pliable dough. Knead for a couple of minutes, but don't overdo it; it just needs to be well mixed and look smooth. Transfer to a clean bowl brushed with a little oil and cover with cling film. Leave to prove until it has doubled in size – about 2 hours in a warm room.

While the dough is proving, heat the olive oil gently in a large, deep frying pan. Sweat the onions and peppers together for 15 minutes until starting to soften, then add the garlic, paprika and sherry vinegar. Continue to cook for about an hour until you have a softly melting mass – the longer and slower you do this the sweeter the result, so take your time. Stir through the parsley and season to taste with salt and pepper. Gently fold through the tuna, trying not to break it up too much. Turn off the heat and set aside to cool.

Preheat the oven to 220°C/200°C Fan/Gas Mark 7. Once the dough has risen, turn it out on to a lightly oiled worktop and chop into 12 even-sized pieces. Roll each piece out to a circle about 5mm thick. Add a little pile of cooled filling to one half of each circle, leaving a generous 2cm margin around the edge. Top each with a couple of slices of hard-boiled egg and bring the empty half of the pastry up and over the filling, encasing it completely and crimping the edges together to seal. Brush with a little beaten egg and scatter over a few flakes of sea salt.

Spread the *empanadillas* over a couple of baking trays and bake in the oven for about 20–25 minutes, until the crust is golden and crisp.

The quintessential Spanish street breakfast, *churros* are long, thin doughnuts served with a rich chocolate sauce for dunking. You could also flavour the sauce the Mexican way with a little orange zest stirred through as the milk warms.

CHURROS AND CHOCOLATE SAUCE

SERVES 4–6

375g self-raising flour
a pinch of salt
600ml boiling water
3 tablespoons olive oil
2 teaspoons vanilla extract
150g caster sugar
2 teaspoons ground cinnamon

for the sauce
300ml milk
100g milk chocolate, chopped
100g dark chocolate, chopped
2 teaspoons cornflour

you will need
a piping bag fitted with a 1cm
    star nozzle

Stir the flour and salt together in a large bowl. Pour in the boiling water, olive oil and vanilla extract and beat together thoroughly to form a smooth paste. Set aside to rest for 10 minutes, then spoon the dough into a piping bag fitted with a star nozzle.

For the sauce, pour the milk into a saucepan, set over a medium heat and bring to simmering point. Remove 1 tablespoon of warm milk and stir it through the cornflour in a small bowl. Add the chocolate to the pan and stir until melted, then pour in the cornflour and milk paste and whisk continuously until the sauce is smooth and thickened. Keep warm over a very low heat.

Stir the sugar and cinnamon together and spread out in a large flat dish or tray.

Heat the oil in a deep fat fryer to 180°C/350°F. Working carefully, squeeze the dough out into 10–12cm-long strips directly into the hot oil. I find the easiest way to snip off the end of a strip is to simply pinch it off with a clean finger and thumb, but you can also cut them with scissors. Don't add more than 4 or 5 to the oil at once or they will stick together. Fry for 4 minutes until crisp and deep golden brown. Drain briefly on kitchen paper before rolling in the cinnamon sugar while still hot. Repeat until you have used up all the dough.

Serve the *churros* warm with the chocolate sauce to dunk them in.

THE MIDDLE EAST AND AFRICA

Spanning a vast geographical area from European-influenced Turkey down to the tip of South Africa, this is a continent of wonderfully diverse eating opportunities. Middle Eastern and North African specialities like falafel and hummus, *brik a l'oeuf* or barbecued sardines are now familiar to many, but plunge a little deeper and many tasty surprises pop up that will stretch your recipe repertoire in the most delicious way.

Midye dolma is the most unusual recipe for mussels I have ever come across, where each shell is carefully stuffed with subtly-spiced rice before being steamed to perfection. Another treat is the little known Ethiopian speciality, *doro wat*, a fiery stew of chicken and eggs that is so exquisite it deserves shouting about. Or try the spicy *suya* kebabs, a Nigerian barbecued beef with a spicy peanut crust, a roadside speciality that is universally adored.

As with other parts of the world, the movement and migration of people has happily resulted in a delicious cross pollination of cuisines. The Indian influence in South Africa is clearly seen in the world-famous bunny chow, practically the national dish of a spicy curry filled bread roll. The utterly simple masala pineapples are an unusual taste revelation – hot, sweet and delicious – that just has to be tried. In Mauritius, the Indian influence is also clear, with fabulous spilt pea-stuffed *dholl puri* flatbread served with fragrant curries.

Gozleme are incredibly tasty stuffed flatbreads from Turkey. The dough is made with plain yogurt, which makes it a delight to work with: smooth, stretchy and very well behaved. They would usually be cooked on a flat griddle over a wood fire, so in the spirit of tradition I like to fire up my barbecue until it's really hot and bung them on as I fill them. Alternatively, a large flat frying pan will do the job nicely.

GOZLEME WITH SPINACH, FETA AND PINENUTS

MAKES 6 GOZLEME

260g baby leaf spinach, washed, then dried in a salad spinner
200g feta cheese, crumbled
1 small onion
2 tablespoons plain yogurt
50g pinenuts
½ nutmeg, grated
salt and freshly ground black pepper

for the dough
500g plain flour
1 teaspoon fast-action yeast
½ teaspoon salt
100ml boiling water
300g plain yogurt
a drizzle of vegetable oil, for rolling

For the dough, place the flour, yeast and salt in a mixing bowl and stir together. Measure the boiling water into a jug and pour the yogurt on top, mixing together until combined. Pour into the flour, stirring as you go until you have a soft dough. Tip on to a lightly floured worktop and knead until smooth. Divide it into 6 even-sized pieces and knead again briefly before placing on a lightly floured baking tray. Cover with a clean tea towel and leave to prove for 30 minutes, or up to an hour.

Meanwhile, roughly chop the spinach and add to a mixing bowl, scattering the cheese on top. Grate in the onion and add the yogurt. Stir together until evenly combined.

Place the pinenuts in a small frying pan and set over a medium heat. Toast for a minute or two until golden, then add to the filling. Season generously with the nutmeg, salt and pepper.

Drizzle a little oil on to the worktop and roll a ball of dough around in it to get an even coating. Roll the dough out to a thin, roughly circular shape, turning over as you roll to make sure it doesn't stick to the worktop or rolling pin. It should be a few millimetres thick and about 25–28cm in diameter.

Fold the top of the circle down about 3–4cm to straighten the top edge. Repeat with the bottom edge. Spoon about 2–3 tablespoons of filling into the centre, and spread it out to form a rectangle around 12cm wide, avoiding the folded edges at the top and bottom. Bring one side of the dough over the filling, pressing it down at the top and bottom to seal, then bring the other side over that, again pressing down to seal. Turn over so the folds are facing down and lay on a lightly oiled baking tray. Repeat with the other pieces of dough.

Fire up your barbecue until hot if you are going to cook outside – you can cook directly on the bars, or use a flat griddle plate if you have one. Alternatively, set a large frying pan over a high heat if you are cooking inside. Cook the parcels, one or two at a time, for about 3 minutes each side until the bread is crisp and dark in places. You shouldn't need to add any extra oil as they were rolled in oil while being assembled.

Serve immediately, but take care with your first bite as the filling will be very hot.

Literally 'fish bread', this Turkish sandwich is simple, quick and utterly delicious – perfect for an impromptu barbecue. Just make sure your fish is spanking fresh – if ever there was a fish that should be eaten straight from the sea, it's a mackerel.

BALIK EKMEK

SERVES 2; EASILY SCALED UP FOR A CROWD

2 Romano peppers
4 small (or 2 large) mackerel fillets
1 teaspoon sumac
½ teaspoon dried chilli flakes, or to taste
a drizzle of olive oil
2 pieces of baguette, cut to the length of the fish fillets
salt and freshly ground black pepper

to serve
lemon juice, to taste
lettuce
sliced tomato
thinly sliced red onion
mayonnaise (optional)

Fire up your barbecue until it's hot and add the whole peppers to the grill, turning them regularly until they are lightly charred and soft. Depending on the heat, this should take about 10 minutes or so.

Season the mackerel fillets on both sides with a sprinkle of sumac and chilli flakes and a little salt and pepper. Drizzle over just a little olive oil and grill over hot coals for 2–3 minutes on each side, skin-side-down first. Use a fish grilling cage if you have one as there is less chance of the fish sticking and you can turn the fillets over all in one go.

Open out the pieces of baguette, but leave top and bottom hinged together, and lightly toast the cut sides on the grill.

To serve, add a whole pepper to each piece of bread – don't worry about removing the stalk and seeds, simply leave that end poking out of the roll and discard when you eat up to it. Top the pepper with a couple of small mackerel fillets (or 1 large) and squeeze over a little lemon juice. Finally, add a little salad – lettuce, tomato, red onion – and finish with a dollop of mayo, if using. Fold over the top of the bread and tuck in immediately.

This is a really different take on mussels, and a speciality on the streets of Istanbul. The mussels are opened out, stuffed with a spiced rice mixture and then steamed to perfection. Delicious. Opening a mussel does take a little practice, but it's very similar to shucking an oyster. You are essentially slicing the mussel in half, so there will be meat on both sides of the shell – but don't be alarmed if it looks a bit 'butchered'!

MIDYE DOLMA

MAKES AROUND 20–30 STUFFED MUSSELS, SERVING 2–4

80g long grain rice
1 tablespoon olive oil
1 onion
½ teaspoon ground cinnamon
½ teaspoon ground allspice
a pinch of dried chilli flakes
40g pinenuts
40g currants
a handful of flat-leaf parsley, finely chopped
500g fresh live mussels, washed under cold running water, discarding any that don't close on tapping
100ml boiling water
salt and freshly ground black pepper

Soak the long grain rice in cold water for 30 minutes.

Place the olive oil in a medium-sized lidded saucepan and set over a low heat. Stir through the onion, cinnamon, allspice and chilli flakes and cook for about 15 minutes, stirring frequently, until the onion is soft and translucent.

Drain the soaked rice and rinse under cold water before adding to the pan with the spiced onions. Add the pinenuts, currants, parsley and a seasoning of salt and pepper, stirring well to mix. Pour in just enough boiling water to cover the rice by 1cm and bring to the boil. Cover with a tight-fitting lid and boil for 3 minutes, then turn off the heat and leave undisturbed with the lid on for 10 minutes.

Meanwhile, open the mussels on a chopping board with a small sharp knife. The following instructions are for those who are right-handed; you will need to reverse them if you're left-handed. Take a mussel in your left hand, hold it hinge end pointing left and flat edge pointing up towards you. The more curved edge of the mussel is facing down on the board. With the sharp edge of the blade facing to the right, force the tip of the knife directly down about halfway along the side facing up to you and pull the blade to the right and round so it meets the chopping board, giving it a little twist as you go. This should allow you to open the mussel into two still-joined halves. You are trying to break the hinge just enough so that the tension goes and the two halves open, but not so much that they separate. Repeat with all the mussels.

Remove the lid from the rice and fork it through to separate the grains. Take an opened mussel and fill it with a heaped teaspoon of rice mixture, pushing the two halves back together as much as you can. Put the stuffed mussel into a large, deep frying pan, hinge side down, rice facing upwards – you need to try to line up all the mussels in a single layer in the pan.

Once all the mussels are stuffed and in the pan, pour in the boiling water and cover with a tight lid or piece of foil. Set the pan over a medium heat and steam the mussels for 10 minutes, or until the flesh is opaque and cooked through. After about 7–8 minutes, take a peek to see if the water has steamed dry, adding a splash more if it has. These are also great cooked in the same way over a medium-hot barbecue – the temperature is about right if you can comfortably hold your hand 10cm above the heat for around 3 or 4 seconds.

Serve hot, or allow to cool a little – they are just as good served warm.

Looking like a bagel and covered liberally with sesame seeds, *simit* are hugely popular and sold from street carts all over Turkey. Traditionally eaten as a savoury breakfast bread with a lump of feta-like cheese and some tomatoes, they also taste mighty fine with butter and jam. The pekmez date molasses is traditional, but may be hard to source; pomegranate molasses is an ideal substitute.

SIMIT

MAKES 8 SIMIT

750g strong white bread flour
1½ teaspoons fast-action yeast
1 teaspoon fine salt
450ml warm water
a little vegetable oil, for shaping
    the dough
125g sesame seeds
50ml pekmez date molasses, or
    pomegranate molasses

Add the flour, yeast and salt to a food mixer fitted with a dough hook and stir briefly to mix. With the motor running slowly, gently pour in the water and mix to a fairly stiff dough. Knead until smooth and elastic, about 8–10 minutes. You can also make this by hand, kneading for a few minutes longer to get a smooth, stretchy dough.

Transfer the dough to a clean, lightly oiled mixing bowl, cover with cling film and set aside to prove until doubled in size. This will take an hour or two at room temperature, or you can prove it overnight in the fridge.

When the dough has risen, tip it on to a lightly oiled worktop and chop into 16 even-sized pieces. Take 1 piece and roll it into a long sausage shape about 1.5cm thick. Repeat with another piece of dough, then twist the two lengths around each other like a rope. Bring the two ends of the rope together and press firmly to join, shaping into a circular ring, much like a bagel, and lay on a baking tray. Repeat with the remaining dough to give you 8 *simit* in total, spread out over a couple of baking trays.

Tip the sesame seeds into a flat, wide bowl, and mix the pekmez (or pomegranate molasses) and 50ml water in another wide bowl. Take a *simit* and dip one side into the thinned pekmez, give it a shake to get rid of excess moisture, then dip the wet side into the sesame seeds to get an even coating. Return to the baking tray, sesame side up, and repeat with the other 7. Set aside to prove for 10–15 minutes while you preheat the oven.

Heat the oven to 220°C/200°C Fan/Gas Mark 7.

Slide the trays into the oven and bake for 20 minutes until deep golden brown. These are best served warm from the oven.

Homemade falafels are fabulous as you can add herbs and spices that are so often sadly lacking in the ready made ones. By stuffing them into a pitta with hummus and salad you have a full and satisfying meal, perfect for on-the-go eating.

Note: you will need to begin this recipe the night before you want to eat, as the chickpeas need to soak overnight.

FALAFEL PITTAS WITH HUMMUS AND CHOPPED SALAD

SERVES 6

500g dried chickpeas
1 small onion, roughly chopped
2 garlic cloves, crushed
a small bunch of coriander, roughly chopped
a small bunch of flat-leaf parsley, roughly chopped
1 tablespoon cumin seeds
1 tablespoon coriander seeds
1–2 teaspoons dried chilli flakes (optional)
4 tablespoons plain flour
1 heaped teaspoon baking powder
salt and freshly ground black pepper
6 large pitta breads, toasted and sliced open
hot chilli sauce (optional)

for the hummus
1 teaspoon bicarbonate of soda
160g light tahini
3 garlic cloves, crushed
juice of ½ lemon, or to taste
6–7 tablespoons cold water

for the salad
250g cherry tomatoes, finely diced
3 spring onions, thinly sliced
½ cucumber, finely diced
a small handful of both coriander and flat-leaf parsley, finely chopped
2 tablespoons olive oil
a splash of red wine vinegar, to taste

Soak the chickpeas overnight in plenty of cold water (at least double their volume).

Drain the chickpeas well and weigh into a bowl; they should have approximately doubled in weight. Add 750g of the chickpeas to a food processor – these will become the falafels. Add the onion, garlic and herbs and pulse until you have a crumbly mixture.

Place the cumin, coriander and chilli, if using, into a small frying pan and dry fry for a minute over a high heat until you can smell their aroma wafting up from the pan. Tip into a pestle and mortar and grind roughly before adding to the food processor. Add the flour, 4 tablespoons cold water, baking powder and a generous seasoning of salt and pepper, then pulse again until it forms a coarse paste. Tip into a bowl and chill in the fridge for an hour. This lets the flavours develop and allows the chickpeas to soak in the moisture. Wash and dry the food processor.

While the falafel mix is resting, make the hummus. Tip the remaining chickpeas into a large saucepan. Sprinkle over the bicarbonate of soda and cover well with fresh cold water. Set the pan over a medium-high heat and bring to the boil, cooking for 25–35 minutes, until tender.

Drain the chickpeas and tip into the clean food processor, along with the tahini, garlic and lemon juice. Process until you have a coarse paste. With the motor running, start to add the cold water, a tablespoon at a time, until the hummus is as smooth as you want it to be. I like mine as smooth as possible, but process for a little less time if you like it coarser. Season to taste with salt and pepper, and a squeeze more lemon juice if you like, and scrape into a bowl. Set aside to rest while you continue with the falafels.

Heat the oil in a deep fat fryer to 180°C/350°F. Take tablespoonfuls of the falafel mixture and roll into balls about the size of a walnut. You need to press and squeeze the mixture together really firmly so it doesn't crumble during cooking; using slightly wet hands helps prevent too much stickiness. Repeat with the rest of the mixture, lining them up on a baking tray. Fry in batches in the hot oil for 4–5 minutes, until deeply golden and crisp, draining on kitchen paper as you go.

Combine all the salad ingredients together in a bowl, seasoning to taste with a little salt and pepper.

To serve, spread a generous spoonful or two of hummus inside an open pitta bread; top with a few falafels, a little salad and a drizzle of chilli sauce, if using.

Popular in Israel and Lebanon, *kibbeh* are crisp, torpedo-shaped croquettes made of bulgur wheat, minced beef and spices. They are a bit of a fiddle to make but very much worth it. They also freeze well in their shaped but unfried state, so make sure you save some for when you don't have the time to make them.

KIBBEH WITH LEMON TAHINI

MAKES ABOUT 8 LARGE KIBBEH, SERVING 6–8

250g bulgur wheat
50g pinenuts
2 tablespoons olive oil, plus a drizzle to garnish
1 medium onion, finely chopped
1 teaspoon allspice berries, ground
1 tablespoon cumin seeds
400g minced beef or lamb
salt and freshly ground black pepper
chopped parsley, smoked paprika and lemon wedges, to garnish

for the lemon tahini sauce
150g light tahini
3 tablespoons olive oil
juice and zest of 1 lemon
1 garlic clove, crushed

Place the bulgur wheat in a heatproof bowl and pour over enough boiling water to cover by 5mm. Cover the bowl with cling film and set aside for 20 minutes to allow the bulgur wheat to absorb the water.

Meanwhile, add the pinenuts to a large frying pan and set over a medium heat. Toast for a minute or two until golden, making sure they don't burn. Tip into a small bowl and set aside. Lower the heat and add the olive oil and half the onion to the frying pan, frying gently for 10 minutes until the onion is just starting to soften. Turn the heat up to medium-high and add the allspice and cumin seeds, stirring well to mix. Add 300g of the mince, season generously with salt and pepper and fry for a good 10 minutes, stirring regularly to break up the meat. Turn off the heat, stir through the pinenuts and allow to cool.

Add the soaked bulgur wheat, a handful at a time, to a food processor, whizzing it well between additions. You need to grind the bulgur so it's almost dough-like, and this is achieved more easily by not overloading the machine. Once all the bulgur is ground, add the rest of the raw mince and the remaining chopped onion. Season generously with salt and pepper and continue to process to a dough-like consistency. It needs to be pliable enough to shape and fill, so if it's a little dry add a splash of ice-cold water and process again.

To shape the *kibbeh*, take a tablespoon of the bulgur mixture and roll it into an egg shape. Use your thumb to press a deep hollow down the centre of the 'egg', then fill the hollow with a couple of teaspoons of cold filling. Squeeze the sides and top together to re-form the *kibbeh* into an egg shape, with the filling completely enclosed. Set aside on a tray. Repeat with the remaining bulgur and filling mixtures; washing your hands regularly and keeping them damp while you shape the *kibbeh* will reduce the stickiness. If you wish to freeze a batch, place them on a baking tray to freeze initially, then pack into a bag or tub and leave in the freezer until ready to cook.

Make the lemon tahini sauce by placing all the ingredients in a deep jug with 150ml cold water and whizz to a smooth, creamy sauce using a stick blender. Season to taste with salt and pepper and set aside.

Heat the oil in a deep fat fryer to 180°C/350°F. Fry the *kibbeh* in batches for about 6 minutes until a deep golden brown. Drain briefly over kitchen paper. If cooking from frozen, add a couple of minutes to the cooking time, and check that they are piping hot all the way through before serving.

To serve, spread a couple of tablespoons of lemon tahini sauce on to a plate and sprinkle with a little parsley and smoked paprika. Top with 2–3 hot *kibbeh*, add a wedge of lemon and serve immediately with a drizzle of olive oil.

The national dish of Egypt, and sold from street carts throughout the land, *koshari* – with two types of pasta, rice *and* lentils – is a carb lover's dream. Very tasty and filling, this is a really authentic and economical street food dish. Do as the *koshari* sellers do and have everything lined up in bowls, ready to mix, heat and serve in an instant. I cook my rice with chicken or vegetable stock for the added flavour, but use water if you prefer.

KOSHARI

SERVES 4–6

200g basmati rice
200g brown or green lentils
100g dried macaroni
6 tablespoons olive oil
3 large onions, finely sliced
75g rice vermicelli, broken into
    1cm pieces
1 tablespoon cumin seeds
1 teaspoon ground cinnamon
500ml chicken or vegetable
    stock, or water
salt and freshly ground black
    pepper
chopped coriander, to garnish

for the tomato sauce
1 tablespoon cumin seeds
1–2 teaspoons dried chilli flakes,
    to taste
2 tablespoons olive oil
4 garlic cloves, crushed
2 x 400g cans plum tomatoes,
    chopped
1 tablespoon vinegar (red wine,
    cider or sherry)
1 teaspoon granulated sugar

Soak the basmati rice in cold water for an hour.

For the tomato sauce, place the cumin seeds and chilli in a large saucepan and set over a medium-high heat. As soon as the spices smell toasty and aromatic – after a minute or so – pour in the oil, garlic and tomatoes, along with 350ml water, the vinegar and the sugar. Season well with salt and pepper, bring to the boil and reduce the heat to a steady simmer. Cook uncovered for about 30 minutes until thick and rich.

Add the lentils to a large saucepan and cover with cold water. Bring to the boil and simmer until just tender but not mushy, about 20–25 minutes. Drain and set aside. Add the macaroni to a saucepan, pour over boiling water to cover it generously and boil until just tender, about 10 minutes. Drain and set aside.

Set a large frying pan over a medium-low heat. Add the oil and sliced onions and fry gently until a deep golden brown, at least 30–40 minutes. Stir every now and then to ensure even cooking, and more frequently towards the end of the cooking time. Use a slotted spoon to scoop out the onions into a dish, leaving as much oil in the pan as you can. Set the onions aside.

Add the vermicelli to the pan, stir frying until golden, about 3 minutes or so. Then add the cumin and cinnamon along with the drained rice, stirring well to coat it in the oil. Pour in the stock, season with salt and pepper, and bring to the boil, then reduce the heat to a steady simmer. Cover with a tight-fitting lid or snugly tucked-in piece of foil, and cook for 10 minutes, then turn off the heat and leave undisturbed (no peeking under the lid) for a further 10 minutes. Remove the lid and lightly fork through the cooked lentils and macaroni. Taste to check the seasoning, adding a little more if necessary.

Serve the *koshari* hot or warm with the warmed tomato sauce on top, scattered with the fried onions and a generous handful of coriander.

Ful medames is a hearty fava bean purée common all over the Middle East, but especially in Egypt and Syria where it's a regular street breakfast dish. The Egyptians favour serving it with chopped tomato and boiled egg; the Syrians with tahini, olive oil and Aleppo pepper sauce. Here I've gone the whole hog and served it with both for a satisfying and very pretty-looking brunch.

Note: you will need to begin this recipe the night before you want to eat, as the beans need to soak overnight.

FUL MEDAMES WITH LEMON TAHINI AND ALEPPO PEPPER

SERVES 4–6

300g split dried fava beans
2 tablespoons olive oil
1 red or white onion, finely chopped
1 garlic clove, crushed
1 tablespoon cumin seeds
juice of ½ lemon, or to taste
1 tablespoon Aleppo chilli flakes
2 tablespoons boiling water
6 ripe vine tomatoes, chopped
3 eggs, hard-boiled, peeled and quartered
1 quantity of lemon tahini sauce (page 136)
olive oil, for drizzling
lemon wedges, to serve
a handful of flat-leaf parsley, chopped, to serve
salt and freshly ground black pepper

Soak the fava beans overnight in cold water, then drain.

Add the oil and onion to a large saucepan and set over a medium heat, frying for about 10 minutes until the onion is beginning to soften. Add the garlic and cumin seeds and fry for a further minute before adding the drained fava beans. Pour over 1.5 litres of cold fresh water and bring to the boil, then reduce the heat to a steady simmer. Cook, uncovered, for about 1½ hours, by which time the beans should be soft and collapsing and most of the water absorbed. Stir regularly, especially towards the end of cooking, as it will be prone to sticking. Stir through lemon juice to taste and season generously with salt and pepper.

While the beans are cooking, place the Aleppo chilli flakes into a small heatproof glass bowl and pour over the boiling water. Set aside at room temperature for an hour or so until the chilli is rehydrated. Stir to mix just before serving.

To serve, divide the beans between shallow dishes. Scatter the tomatoes around the edge and tuck in a few pieces of boiled egg. Pour a little of the lemon tahini sauce over the beans and drizzle over plenty of olive oil and a little of the chilli sauce, add a lemon wedge to the plate too. Sprinkle with parsley and tuck in.

This Tunisian crisp fried parcel is packed with flavours, and fits the bill perfectly as an indulgent, solo-eating, speedy street food snack. I've included my favourite recipe for homemade harissa, as the complex flavours surpass the ready made stuff, and it's a really useful thing to have lurking in your fridge.

BRIK A L'OEUF WITH CHICKPEAS AND HARISSA

SERVES 1; EASILY SCALED UP FOR A CROWD

30 x 50cm sheet of filo pastry
50g cooked chickpeas
1 large egg
1 tablespoon chopped coriander
5g butter, melted
salt and freshly ground black pepper
a wedge of lemon, to serve

for the harissa
1 large red pepper
200g medium-hot fresh red chillies, roughly chopped
4 garlic cloves, chopped
6 tablespoons olive oil
3 heaped teaspoons caraway seeds, roughly ground
3 heaped teaspoons cumin seeds, roughly ground
1 tablespoon tomato purée
1 tablespoon red wine vinegar
2 tablespoons smoked paprika

For the harissa, blacken the skin of the red pepper: the easiest way to do this is to hold it over a gas flame using long-handled tongs, turning until crisp and black all over. You can also do it under a really hot grill, turning frequently. Put the blackened pepper into a bowl, cover tightly with cling film and allow to cool.

Once cool enough to handle, peel and deseed the pepper, then roughly chop the flesh, placing it in a food processor as you go. Add the chillies, garlic, oil, caraway, cumin, tomato purée, red wine vinegar and paprika and a generous seasoning of salt and pepper. Process until really smooth before scraping into a bowl. The harissa will keep for 2 weeks or more in the fridge with a layer of cling film pressed to the surface to keep the air out, and it freezes brilliantly too.

To make the *brik*, preheat the oil in a deep fat fryer to 180°C/350°F.

Lay the sheet of filo on the worktop and spread a dollop of harissa in the centre. Sprinkle on the chickpeas in a rough ring of about 9–10cm diameter and crack the egg into the middle (the chickpeas create a sort of wall, stopping the egg from running all over the place). Sprinkle over the coriander and season with a little salt and pepper. Fold one side of the pastry over the egg, followed by the opposite side, so the filling is completely covered, then fold over the bottom edge, brush with the melted butter, and fold the top down to create a neat parcel.

Carefully add to the hot oil, fold-side-down first to seal it, and fry for about 4 minutes, turning over halfway through. If you like your egg yolk a little more set, increase the cooking time by a minute. Drain briefly on kitchen paper before squeezing over a little lemon juice and tucking in while still piping hot.

These delicious fried rolls are filled with mechouia salad – a spicy grilled and chopped vegetable salad, with tuna, eggs and olives, traditionally served in Tunisia. For the very best flavour, grill the vegetables over a hot barbecue. The recipe makes double what you need to fill the rolls, but it keeps well for several days in the fridge and makes a lovely dip.

FRICASSEE TUNISIENNE WITH MECHOUIA SALAD

MAKES 12 BITE-SIZED SANDWICHES, SERVES 6 ALLOWING 2 EACH

5 large vine tomatoes, stems on
4 green chillies
2 red peppers
4 garlic cloves, unpeeled
1 large red onion, unpeeled, cut into wedges through the root
2 teaspoons caraway seeds
2 teaspoons cumin seeds
50ml olive oil
juice of ½–1 lemon, to taste
250g good-quality tuna fish (preferably packed in olive oil), drained
3 hard-boiled eggs, peeled and sliced
12 pitted black olives, sliced
a little flat-leaf parsley, chopped
salt and freshly ground black pepper

for the fricassee rolls
300g strong white bread flour
1 teaspoon salt
½ teaspoon fast-action yeast
1 teaspoon runny honey
1 egg
150ml warm water
oil, for kneading

To make the *fricassee* rolls, place the flour, salt, yeast, honey and egg in the bowl of a food mixer. With the dough hook attached, start the motor slowly and gradually pour in the water. Increase the speed of the motor and knead for 5 minutes until you have a smooth, soft dough. Scrape into a lightly oiled bowl and cover with cling film. Set aside to prove until doubled in size – about an hour or two, depending on the warmth of your kitchen.

Once the dough has risen, tip on to a lightly oiled worktop and knead briefly. Chop into 12 even-sized pieces, rolling each into a little torpedo shape. Leave to rest, well spaced out over one or two lightly oiled baking trays. Loosely cover with a clean tea towel and leave to prove for another hour.

While the rolls are proving, fire up a barbecue or set a griddle pan over a high heat. Add the whole tomatoes, chillies and peppers and cook until charred all over, turning regularly. Add to a bowl and cover with cling film to loosen the skins ready for peeling. Add the garlic cloves to the grill and cook until soft and the skin charred. Finally, add the onion wedges and cook until starting to soften and lightly charred. When all the vegetables are cooked, allow them to cool a little so you can handle them comfortably.

Peel and discard the tomato, chilli and red pepper skins and deseed the peppers and chillies. Finely chop the flesh and add to a bowl. Squeeze the garlic cloves from their skins and mash the flesh, adding it to the bowl with the vegetables. Discard the outer skin of the onions and the root and finely chop, then add it to the bowl.

Toast the caraway and cumin seeds in a small frying pan over a medium heat for a couple of minutes until you can smell their aroma wafting up from the pan. Tip into a spice mill or pestle and mortar and grind roughly. Add to the bowl with the other ingredients. Pour in the olive oil and season with lemon juice, salt and pepper, gently stirring everything together. Set aside at room temperature.

Once the rolls have proved, heat the oil in a deep fat fryer to 180°C/350°F. Fry the rolls in batches for 4–5 minutes, turning halfway through, until deeply golden brown. Drain briefly on kitchen paper before splitting open, ready to fill.

Add a couple of teaspoons of mechouia salad to each roll. Top with a little tuna, a slice of egg and some slices of olive. Finally sprinkle in a little parsley before pressing shut. Serve at room temperature. The rolls will keep well for an hour or so after filling.

In its native Morocco, this tasty soup is often eaten as a hearty workers' breakfast, served from street stalls and hole-in-the-wall cafés. With such a simple pulse-based dish, getting the seasoning right is absolutely key to elevating it from potentially bland to really sublime, and here a sprinkle of spice and a good drizzle of lemon and garlic oil make this soup sing.

BESSARA WITH CUMIN AND LEMON AND GARLIC OIL

SERVES 4–6

200ml olive oil, plus an extra 2 tablespoons
rind of 1 large lemon
6 garlic cloves: 3 sliced, 3 crushed
3 tablespoons cumin seeds
2 teaspoons dried chilli flakes
1 large onion, chopped
350g dried split peas (green or yellow)
1.75 litres vegetable stock
salt and freshly ground black pepper

Make the lemon and garlic oil by adding 200ml olive oil, the lemon rind and the sliced garlic to a small, heavy-based saucepan set over a low heat. Allow the oil to warm very, very gently for 30 minutes. It should not boil, just slowly putter away with the odd tiny bubble breaking the surface. Remove from the heat and leave to infuse until you are ready to serve.

In a large, heavy-based saucepan, toast the cumin seeds and chilli flakes over a medium-low heat. As soon as you can smell their aroma wafting up from the pan, tip them into a pestle and mortar and grind coarsely.

Place 2 tablespoons olive oil in a pan along with the onion and set over a low heat to soften gently without colouring. This will take a good 30 minutes, so be patient. When the onion is meltingly soft, add the crushed garlic and half of the ground spices and cook for a further couple of minutes.

Add the split peas, pour over the stock and bring to the boil. Reduce the heat a little and simmer steadily until the peas are soft and collapsing. Purée the soup until velvety smooth, using either a stick blender or a liquidiser. Season to taste with salt and pepper and keep warm over a low heat.

Strain the lemon and garlic oil through a fine sieve and discard the lemon rind and garlic slices. The oil will keep in a clean covered jar for at least a couple of weeks.

Serve the soup in deep bowls or mugs, sprinkled with the remaining spices and drizzled with the lemon and garlic oil.

Herrings are like the big cousins of sardines and with a little more flesh to the bone they are less fiddly to eat. You could very easily substitute sardines if they are easier to find, however. Either way, just make sure your fish are spanking fresh in this simple barbecue recipe with a Moroccan street food twist.

GRILLED CHERMOULA HERRINGS

SERVES 4

5 tablespoons olive oil
finely grated zest and juice of 1 lemon
1½ tablespoons ground coriander
1 teaspoon smoked paprika
1 teaspoon ground cumin
1 teaspoon ground ginger
a small bunch of coriander, roughly chopped
8 medium-sized herrings (about 1.2kg), gutted and cleaned
salt and freshly ground black pepper

Make the chermoula by mixing everything except the herrings together in a small bowl. Season to taste with salt and pepper.

Make a few slashes through the skin of the herrings and rub a little salt and pepper all over them. Add a spoonful of chermoula into the gut cavity of each fish and rub a little all over the outside of each. Set aside to marinate for about 30 minutes, or up to an hour.

Preheat your barbecue to medium-hot – the temperature is about right if you can comfortably hold your hand 10cm above the heat for around 3–4 seconds. Grill the herrings on the barbecue for about 4 minutes each side until cooked through and crisp on the outside.

Beghrir, also known as 'thousand hole pancakes', are a hybrid between a crumpet and an American pancake and are popular in Morocco as a breakfast on the run, or as a snack to break fasting during Ramadan. I love to eat these with fresh figs – their musky sweetness feels like a fitting match with the honey butter syrup – but raspberries or a few blueberries would be good too.

BEGHRIR WITH HONEY BUTTER SYRUP

MAKES 10–12, SERVING ABOUT 4

150g plain flour
150g semolina
2 teaspoons baking powder
1 teaspoon fast-action yeast
1 teaspoon caster sugar
½ teaspoon fine salt
250ml milk
250ml warm water
a little vegetable oil, for frying
4 fresh figs, quartered, to serve
  (optional)

for the honey butter syrup
100g honey
100g butter
1 teaspoon orange blossom
  water (optional)

Place the flour, semolina, baking powder, yeast, caster sugar and salt in a food processor and pulse to mix. With the motor running, slowly pour in the milk, followed by the water, and mix until you have a smooth, thin batter. Alternatively, mix the dry ingredients together in a large bowl before pouring in the milk and water, whisking all the time until smooth. Leave to rest at room temperature for 30 minutes.

To make the syrup, place the honey, butter and orange blossom water, if using, in a small saucepan and set over a low heat to melt, mixing thoroughly until you have a smooth, buttery syrup. Keep warm.

Once the batter has rested, heat a tiny drizzle of oil in a frying pan set over a medium-high heat. Once it's really hot, scrunch up a piece of kitchen paper and spread the oil out in a very thin, even layer over the base of the pan. Add a ladleful of batter to the pan and swirl around to a flat circular pancake of about 12–14cm in diameter. Cook for a minute or so, until you see (literally) thousands of tiny bubbles rising to the surface. Once the top has lost its wet look, use a fish slice to flip over and cook the other side for just a few seconds to seal it. Transfer to a plate and keep warm. Repeat with the remaining batter – you should get around 10–12 *beghrir*. If there are not enough bubbles it could mean that your pan isn't hot enough , that the batter is too thick (add another tablespoon or so of warm water), or that it just hasn't proved for long enough (leave for another 15 minutes next time).

Serve with the figs alongside, if using, and the honey butter syrup in a jug for drizzling.

Supposedly named 'red red' after its two principal rouge-coloured components – African red palm oil and tomato purée – this is a hearty vegetarian bean stew from Ghana. For the red palm oil, try Afro-Caribbean food shops or online, but if you can't get hold of it, substitute groundnut oil. The finished dish will, however, be red only in the singular.

Note: if you are using dried beans, you will need to begin this recipe the night before you want to eat, as the beans need to soak overnight.

RED RED WITH FRIED PLANTAIN

SERVES 6

375g dried black-eye beans, or 3 x 400g cans, drained and rinsed
100g African red palm oil
2 red onions, chopped
6 garlic cloves, crushed
3cm piece fresh root ginger, grated
1 tablespoon sweet paprika
2 Scotch bonnet chillies, left whole
3 tablespoons tomato purée
400ml vegetable stock
2 or 3 ripe but firm plantains (skin should be mottled equally black and yellow)
vegetable or groundnut oil, for frying
salt and freshly ground black pepper, plus extra sea salt flakes for sprinkling
4 spring onions, finely sliced, to garnish

If using dried beans, soak the beans overnight in plenty of cold water. The following day, drain the soaked beans and add to a large pan. Cover well with cold water and set over a medium-high heat. Bring to the boil and simmer until cooked through, about 25–40 minutes. Drain and set aside.

Meanwhile, add the palm oil to a large, heavy-based pan and set over a medium heat to melt. Add the onions and stir fry until translucent and lightly caramelized, about 20 minutes. Stir through the garlic, ginger, paprika, Scotch bonnet chillies and tomato purée and stir fry for 5 minutes until dark and fragrant. Tip in the cooked or canned beans and season well with salt and pepper. Pour in the stock and bring to a simmer. Simmer steadily, stirring every now and then for about 20 minutes until the stew is rich and thick.

While the stew is simmering, fry the plantains. Peel them and cut on the diagonal into 1cm-thick slices. Take a large frying pan and add a good few tablespoons of oil. Set over a medium-high heat and, once the oil is hot, add the plantain slices in a single layer. Don't overcrowd the pan: you may need to cook them in a couple of batches. Fry for about 2 minutes each side until golden and crisp. Drain over kitchen paper, sprinkle with sea salt and keep warm in a low oven (around 110°C/90°C Fan/Gas Mark ¼) until the stew is ready.

Taste to check the seasoning, adding more salt or pepper if needed. Serve the stew hot or warm, scattered with the spring onions and with the fried plantains on the side.

With the peanuts and spices, I guess these kebabs are the African equivalent of Indonesian satay. Except here the peanuts are ground to a powder and rubbed all over the meat rather than turned into a dipping sauce. The chicken stock cube may seem like an odd addition, but it's really authentic and *suya* just wouldn't be *suya* without it.

Note: you will need to begin this recipe the day before you want to eat, if you wish to marinate the beef overnight.

BEEF SUYA

SERVES 6

750g beef steak (I use skirt, my favourite steak cut, but sirloin, rump or ribeye are all good), sliced across the grain into 1cm strips
1 tablespoon vegetable or groundnut oil
1 lemon, cut into wedges, to serve

for the suya rub
4 tablespoons unsalted peanuts
2 teaspoons chilli powder (or to taste)
1 tablespoon white pepper, preferably freshly ground
1 tablespoon garlic powder
1 tablespoon onion powder
1 chicken stock cube, crumbled
1 teaspoon smoked paprika
1 teaspoon salt

you will need
12 metal or bamboo skewers (if using bamboo, soak in cold water for an hour before using to prevent them from burning)

For the *suya* rub, place the peanuts in a dry frying pan and set over a medium heat. Toast until a deep golden colour, about 3 minutes, then tip into a spice mill. Pulse until ground, but take care not to over-pulse or they will turn into a paste. Tip the ground peanuts into a bowl and stir through the chilli powder, white pepper, garlic powder, onion powder, crumbled stock cube, paprika and salt. You want the *suya* rub to be an evenly mixed powder.

Sprinkle the *suya* rub on to a large flat plate and roll the beef strips in it, covering them as evenly as possible in the spices. Set on to a plate, cover and chill in the fridge for at least an hour, or overnight if you have time. Discard any leftover rub as it has been in contact with raw meat.

When you are ready to cook, thread the beef on to the skewers and drizzle over a little oil. Fire up your barbecue or griddle pan until hot. Cook the skewers for about 8–10 minutes, turning regularly, until deeply coloured on the outside. Serve immediately with a squeeze of lemon juice.

Nigerian jollof rice is said to be the precursor of the Creole classic jambalaya, and like jambalaya it can contain a wide variety of vegetables and meat, more like a paella. However, this version is pared down to its roots: just red peppers and tomatoes puréed with a few spices in which to cook the rice. It's a simple and comforting dish to eat on its own, and is also a fabulous accompaniment to the beef suya on page 155.

JOLLOF RICE

SERVES 6 AS A SIDE OR 4 AS A MAIN MEAL

400g white rice
6 large vine tomatoes, roughly chopped
2 red peppers, deseeded and roughly chopped
2 red onions, roughly chopped
4 garlic cloves, roughly chopped
5cm piece fresh root ginger, roughly chopped
2 tablespoons vegetable or groundnut oil
2 tablespoons tomato purée
2 bay leaves
2 sprigs of fresh thyme
1–2 Scotch bonnet peppers, left whole
500ml chicken stock
50g butter, to finish
salt and freshly ground black pepper

Soak the rice in plenty of cold water for an hour.

Place the tomatoes, red peppers, onions, garlic and ginger in a food processor and whizz until smooth; you may need to do this in 2 batches, depending on the size of your food processor. Tip into a large saucepan and set over a medium-high heat. Bring to the boil and simmer steadily until all the liquid has evaporated, about 50–60 minutes. It's ready when you can draw a wooden spoon across the base of the pan and the purée holds its shape with no puddles of liquid appearing. Stir regularly, particularly towards the end of cooking when it will be prone to sticking.

Add the oil, tomato purée, bay leaves, thyme and Scotch bonnet pepper and stir fry for 10 minutes until thick and glossy.

Drain the rice, add it to the pan along with the stock, then season with salt and pepper, stirring thoroughly to mix. Bring to the boil, reduce to a simmer and cover with a tight-fitting lid. Cook for 15 minutes, stirring every now and then but without scraping the sticky bits off the bottom – they are a highly prized part of the dish. Turn off the heat, put the butter in a lump on top to melt, and re-cover tightly. Leave to rest for 15 minutes before stirring through and scraping off the caramelised sticky bits with a wooden spatula and folding them through the rice.

This Ethiopian chicken and egg stew is really fragrant thanks to the heady mix of berbere spices and a long, slow cooking time. You can buy ready made berbere spice blends in some supermarkets, but I'd urge you to make your own if you can. It takes no time at all if you have a spice mill, and the taste will be infinitely fresher. This stew is traditionally eaten with the hands only, using a flatbread to scoop up the tender chicken and eggs.

DORO WAT

SERVES 4–6

50g unsalted butter
3 red onions, chopped
8 large chicken thighs, skin on,
    bone in
4 garlic cloves, crushed
3cm piece fresh root ginger,
    grated
2 tablespoons tomato purée
juice of 1 lemon
4 hard-boiled eggs, peeled and
    cut in half
salt and freshly ground black
    pepper
flatbreads, to serve

for the berbere spice blend
1 tablespoon coriander seeds
1 teaspoon fenugreek seeds
6 cardamom pods
½ teaspoon allspice berries
½ teaspoon cloves
1 tablespoon sweet paprika
2–3 teaspoons chilli powder, or
    to taste
1 teaspoon ground ginger
½ teaspoon freshly ground
    nutmeg
1 teaspoon salt

For the berbere spice blend, toast the coriander seeds in a small frying pan for a minute. When they are fragrant, tip into a spice mill and add the fenugreek, cardamom, allspice and cloves and whizz to a powder. Tip into a small bowl and stir through the paprika, chilli powder, ginger, nutmeg and salt.

Take a large, heavy-based pan – ideally wide enough to fit the chicken thighs in a single layer – and set over a low heat. Add the butter and, once melted, add the onions. Cook over a very low heat until the onions are very soft and lightly coloured, about 40–45 minutes – the longer the better in terms of flavour. Raise the heat a little and add the chicken thighs, skin down, and fry for 10 minutes or so until pale golden brown. Turn the thighs skin side up and stir through the garlic, ginger, berbere spice blend and tomato purée and pour over 400ml cold water. Add the lemon juice and season with salt and pepper. Bring to a simmer, cover with a lid and cook gently for an hour.

Remove the lid and continue to simmer for another 45–60 minutes to thicken the sauce. The chicken should now be really tender and coming away from the bone. Add the egg halves, tucking them between the chicken thighs and pressing them into the sauce, and simmer for another 5 minutes or so until they are warmed through. Divide between bowls and serve with the flatbreads as cutlery!

Meet the amazing South African Gatsby sarnie – an Indian-spiced barbecued steak, chip and cheese concoction, all squished into a long baguette made for sharing. You could, in theory, add a little salad as a slightly lame nod to health, but in this double-carb meat feast I think it would pretty much miss the point. Go for broke, I say! I've made this with homemade fries and a fragrant spice powder for maximum taste, but if you need to eat fast use oven fries and ready made garam masala.

THE GATSBY

SERVES ABOUT 4, DEPENDING ON HUNGER!

1 tablespoon vegetable oil
500g beef skirt steak
1 baguette, about 50–60cm long, sliced through, but with top and bottom still hinged together
2 generous handfuls of triple-cooked chips (see page 70), or about 250g oven fries
2 handfuls of grated extra-mature Cheddar (about 150g)
sea salt flakes

for the garam masala
1 tablespoon cumin seeds
1 tablespoon coriander seeds
1 teaspoon fennel seeds
1 teaspoon celery seeds
1 teaspoon black peppercorns
1 teaspoon ground turmeric

If you are making your own garam masala, place the cumin, coriander, fennel, celery and the peppercorns in a small frying pan and set over a medium-high heat to toast. As soon as you can smell their aroma wafting up from the pan, turn off the heat and tip into a spice mill or pestle and mortar. Add the turmeric and grind to a powder.

Brush the vegetable oil over both sides of the steak and sprinkle over 1–2 tablespoons spice powder, rubbing it in well. Set aside to marinate at room temperature for 30 minutes to an hour. Sprinkle a little sea salt over both sides of the steak just before grilling.

Fire up your barbecue until hot, or use a griddle pan on the hob if you prefer. Once hot, grill the steak to your liking – about 3 minutes each side for a medium-rare steak, depending on the thickness.

Once the steak is cooked, transfer to a plate, cover loosely with foil and leave to rest for 10 minutes. Slice into thin strips across the grain for maximum tenderness and spread out along the length of the opened baguette. Sprinkle over the hot chips and cheese, and hinge the baguette shut, squeezing together as best you can. Slice into generous chunks and tuck in while still hot and fresh.

Bunny chow is simply a hollow bread roll stuffed with curry – not made with real bunny, but with tender pieces of stewed lamb. In its native South Africa it is often spooned into large hollowed-out loaves of bread, which are designed to be eaten with your hands – quite a challenge, even for the most dextrous! For ease of eating I prefer to use smaller rolls, so really hungry diners may want more than one.

BUNNY CHOW

SERVES 4–8, ALLOWING 1–2 EACH, DEPENDING ON GREED

2 tablespoons vegetable oil
700g lamb leg steaks, cut into 3cm cubes
2 onions, roughly chopped
3 garlic cloves, chopped
4cm piece fresh root ginger, chopped
1 tablespoon cumin seeds
2 teaspoons fennel seeds
1–2 teaspoons dried chilli flakes, to taste
1 cinnamon stick
4 vine tomatoes, chopped
2 tablespoons garam masala (for homemade see page 160)
550–600g (around 2 large) potatoes, peeled and cut into 3cm cubes
8 large crusty white bread rolls
salt and freshly ground black pepper
a small bunch of coriander, chopped, to garnish
1 small red onion, thinly sliced, to garnish

Place the vegetable oil in a large, heavy-based pan and set over a high heat. When it's hot, brown the lamb in 2 or 3 batches, transferring to a plate as you go. Set aside.

Add the onion, garlic and ginger to a food processor and whizz to a smooth paste, adding a tablespoon or two of cold water to help it along, if necessary.

Lower the heat on the empty pan and add the cumin, fennel, chilli flakes and cinnamon stick, frying for a few seconds until you can smell their aroma wafting up from the pan. Stir through the onion paste and fry for 10 minutes until starting to soften. Return all the meat and any juices to the pan, along with the tomatoes and garam masala. Season with salt and pepper, pour in 500ml water and bring to the boil. Cover with a lid, reduce the heat to low and simmer gently for about an hour, until the meat is nearly tender. Add the potatoes, re-cover and simmer for another 30 minutes or so until the potatoes are cooked.

While the curry is simmering, slice the tops off the bread rolls and scoop out the insides to leave a shell about 1cm thick all round. Reserve the insides for dunking in the curry.

When the curry has finished cooking, divide evenly between the hollow rolls. Garnish with a little coriander and a few onion slices and eat immediately – cutlery optional!

Masala pineapples are so simple – they are literally chunks of ripe, juicy fruit rolled in a special masala spice blend and threaded on to a kebab stick. If you've ever been by the beach in Durban, South Africa, where they are sold on numerous street carts, you'll know the fruit and spice combination makes a very refreshing snack in the summer sunshine. They also make a good pre-dinner snack, perfect with a cold beer.

MASALA PINEAPPLES

MAKES 8 FRUIT KEBABS

1 large pineapple, sweet and ripe

for the masala spice blend
1 teaspoon coriander seeds
1 teaspoon cumin seeds
2 cardamom pods
1cm piece cinnamon stick, or
    ½ teaspoon ground cinnamon
½ teaspoon fenugreek seeds
3 cloves
1 tablespoon paprika
½ teaspoon chilli powder
½ teaspoon ground ginger
1 tablespoon caster sugar
    (optional)

Place the coriander, cumin, cardamom, cinnamon stick, fenugreek and cloves in a small frying pan and dry fry over a medium heat for a minute. Tip into a spice mill or pestle and mortar and grind to a powder. Transfer into a shallow bowl and stir through the paprika, chilli powder and ginger.

Peel and core the pineapple, taking your time to remove all the eyes. Taste a little: you want it to be really sweet. If it's a touch sharp, add a little sugar to your spice blend, stirring well to mix.

Chop the pineapple flesh into 3cm wedges and dust them with a little of the spice blend. Thread the cubes on to kebab sticks and serve immediately. If you have some spice powder left over, it makes a fabulous dusty dip to dunk salted crisps in!

Melktert – literally 'milk tart' in Afrikaans – is a delicious cinnamon-topped custard pie that is hugely popular across South Africa. Not limited to street eating, it's often baked at home, to a recipe passed down through generations, and is also served in bakeries across the land as a delicious snack. I make it in a rectangular tin and cut it into sturdy slices, as I find these much easier to eat in the hand than the more traditional wedge shape.

Note: you will need to begin this recipe several hours before you want to eat, or ideally the day before, as the custard needs time to chill.

MELKTERT

SERVES ABOUT 6

500ml milk
50g butter
3 eggs
150g caster sugar
1 tablespoon cornflour
1 teaspoon vanilla extract
1 heaped teaspoon ground
　cinnamon

for the pastry
180g plain flour
90g butter
25g icing sugar
1 egg
2 tablespoons ice-cold water

you will need
a 20 x 26cm rectangular baking
　tin or a 25cm diameter round
　baking tin

To make the pastry, add the flour, butter and icing sugar to a food processor and pulse to a fine crumb. Add the egg and cold water and pulse again until the mixture is in loose clumps. Do not overwork or the pastry will become tough. Spread out a sheet of cling film on the worktop and tip the pastry crumbs into a pile in the middle. Draw up the sides together on top of the crumbs and press into a ball, twisting the cling film to seal. Chill in the fridge for 30 minutes.

Lightly flour the worktop and roll the pastry to fit your chosen tin, to a thickness of about 5mm. Line the tin, press the pastry well into the corners, trim the edges to fit the tin and prick the base all over with a fork. Chill in the fridge for a further 30 minutes: it's worth doing this if you have time as it reduces the chance of pastry shrinkage.

Preheat the oven to 200°C/180°C Fan/Gas Mark 6.

Line the pastry shell with baking parchment and fill with baking beans. Bake for 25 minutes. Remove the paper and beans and return to the oven for a further 5–10 minutes. The pastry gets no further cooking so it's important it gets completely crisp at this stage. Remove from the oven and allow to cool.

To make the filling, place the milk and butter in a saucepan and bring to boiling point.

Crack the eggs into a bowl, add the sugar, cornflour and vanilla extract and whisk together until completely smooth. Once the milk is just at boiling point, pour it carefully over the sugar and egg mix, stirring all the time until combined. Then pour back into the saucepan, set it over a low heat and allow to thicken, stirring constantly, for 5 minutes.

Pour the custard into the pastry case and allow to go cold. Chill in the fridge to set completely, ideally for several hours or overnight. Dust with the cinnamon and cut into wedges to serve.

Dholl puri are lovely nutritious flatbreads with a thin filling of ground split peas. Cooked until soft and still wrappable, they are the classic accompaniment to this butterbean curry. On the streets of Mauritius they are the number-one street food, and quite right too. Delicious, vegetarian and healthy – what's not to love?

DHOLL PURI WITH BUTTERBEAN CURRY

SERVES 4–6

100g chana dal
½ teaspoon ground turmeric
3 tablespoons vegetable oil
2 large onions, sliced
5 garlic cloves, crushed
5cm piece fresh root ginger, grated
3 large vine tomatoes, chopped
3 sprigs thyme
2 x 400g cans butterbeans, drained and rinsed
juice of ½ lemon, or to taste
salt and freshly ground black pepper
a bunch of coriander, chopped, to garnish

for the dough
500g plain flour, plus a little more for kneading
½ teaspoon ground turmeric
1 teaspoon fine salt
2 tablespoons vegetable oil, plus more for rolling

for the Mauritian curry powder
2 tablespoons coriander seeds
1 tablespoon cumin seeds
2 teaspoons fennel seeds
1 teaspoon fenugreek seeds
1–2 teaspoons dried chilli flakes
6 cloves
3 green cardamom pods
1 teaspoon ground cinnamon, or a 1.5cm piece cinnamon stick
½ teaspoon ground turmeric

Place the chana dal and half the turmeric in a saucepan and cover well with cold water. Set over a medium-high heat, bring to the boil and simmer until tender, about 30 minutes. The chana dal need to be soft enough to squash between finger and thumb but not so soft that they collapse, so start testing after about 25 minutes. Drain well and spread out on a large plate or tray, and leave to steam dry until cool. Once cool, add to a food processor and grind to a crumbly powder. Add a pinch of salt and pulse to mix. Set aside.

For the Mauritian curry powder, place the coriander, cumin, fennel, fenugreek and chilli flakes in a small dry frying pan and set over a medium heat. Toast for a minute or two until fragrant then tip into a pestle and mortar or spice mill. Add the cloves, cardamom, cinnamon and turmeric and grind to a powder. Set aside.

For the curry, place the oil and onions in a large saucepan and set over a medium heat for 10 minutes, stirring occasionally until starting to soften and lightly caramelise. Add the garlic and ginger, followed by the Mauritian curry powder, and stir well to mix. Allow to cook for a couple of minutes before adding the tomatoes and stir frying for a further 10 minutes. Pour in 500ml water, tuck in the thyme and season with a little salt and pepper. Cover with a lid and simmer steadily for 20 minutes. Remove the lid and stir through the butterbeans, then simmer for another 10 minutes until thick and rich. Squeeze in the lemon juice, and taste to check seasoning, adding more salt, pepper or lemon juice if you like. Keep warm while you make the *dholl puri*.

To make the dough, tip the flour into a large bowl and add the turmeric and salt, mixing together. Add the oil and 300ml water, stirring to form a dough. Tip on to a lightly floured worktop and knead for 5 minutes, adding a little shake more flour if it seems to be too sticky. Set aside in a bowl to rest for 5 minutes.

Lightly flour the worktop and have the ground chana dal and a dessertspoon handy. Tip the dough on to the floured surface and chop it into 8 even-sized pieces, rolling each into a ball as you go. Take one ball and cup it in the palm of one hand. Take the other hand and, using thumb and forefinger, push a hole in the centre and pinch outwards to form a palm-sized bowl (just like making a pinch pot with clay).

Take a generous dessertspoon of chana dal and use it to fill the hole in the dough. Pinch the edges over the top to close and roll gently between your palms so you have a smooth round ball. Place on a well-floured baking tray, seam side down, and repeat with the remaining 7 pieces of dough. Reserve any leftover chana dal for garnish.

When you are ready to eat, take a large flat frying pan and set over a medium-high heat to warm up. Meanwhile, lightly oil the worktop and roll out one of the balls of dough until you have a round disc about 5mm thick, turning through a quarter turn after each roll to keep it circular. Carefully place in the hot pan and cook for a minute on each side before transferring to a clean plate. While it's cooking, roll out the second *dholl puri* and have it ready to go in the pan as soon as the first one is out. Repeat the rolling and cooking process until they are all cooked.

Scatter the coriander and reserved chana dal over the butterbean curry and serve with the warm *dholl puri*, tearing them into pieces to scoop up the curry.

THE INDIAN SUBCONTINENT

India does street food brilliantly with all regions having their own speciality dishes, and from the smallest village to the biggest city you can be sure of finding something delicious on every corner. From breakfast, lunch and dinner to a myriad of tasty snacks in between, you could quite happily eat your way around this continent without once stepping inside a restaurant.

In the northern city of Kolkata, you just have to try *kati* rolls, a whole meal inside a chapati, consisting of a spiced kebab snugly wrapped in an omelette drizzled in spicy chutney, whilst down in the south the wheat wrap is swapped for the fermented rice and lentil pancake of the *masala dosa*. The island of Sri Lanka has a bit of a thing for coconut and two of their most popular street foods – the now world-famous egg hoppers, and the less well known shrimp *vadai* with *pol sambol* – certainly make the best of it.

Where India seems to truly excel is in delightful snacks, or *'chaat'*, and my favourite is without a doubt *papdi chaat*, the Indian version of nachos, a colourful dish featuring layer upon layer of different flavours and textures that make it pretty much a meal in itself. Some *chaat* make perfect little bar snacks – try Druv Baker's awesome pakoras or the funkily named chicken 65 and it's clear these dishes were pretty much invented to accompany your chosen tipple.

Seekh kebabs are made with finely processed minced meat so they have a smooth, almost pâté-like texture. Traditionally made in Pakistan with lamb, but beef mince works brilliantly too, if you prefer.

SEEKH KEBABS WITH MINT RAITA

MAKES 8 KEBABS, SERVING 4–6

1 tablespoon cumin seeds
1 tablespoon garam masala (for homemade, see page 160)
500g minced lamb or beef
1 medium onion, roughly chopped
25g piece fresh root ginger, grated
3 garlic cloves, roughly chopped
2–3 hot green chillies, to taste
a small bunch of coriander, roughly chopped
1 egg
salt and freshly ground black pepper
vegetable oil, for frying and greasing
naan bread, to serve
lemon wedges, to serve

for the mint raita
4 heaped tablespoons plain yogurt
2 garlic cloves, crushed
a small bunch of both mint leaves and fresh coriander
2–3 green chillies, finely chopped, to taste
juice of 1 lime

you will need
8 metal or bamboo skewers (if using bamboo, soak in cold water for an hour before using to prevent them from burning)

Place the cumin seeds in a dry frying pan and toast for a minute. As soon as you smell their aroma wafting up from the pan, tip into a spice mill or pestle and mortar and grind to a powder. Add to a food processor along with the garam masala, minced meat, onion, ginger, garlic, chillies, coriander and egg. Season generously with salt and pepper and process to a smooth paste. Take a small teaspoon of the mixture and flatten it into a mini patty, then fry in a little oil until cooked through. Taste to check the seasoning and add a little more spice, chilli, salt or pepper if necessary and process once more until combined.

Divide this mixture into 8 even-sized balls. To shape the kebabs, flatten and roll each ball into a cigar shape of about 2cm thickness. Hold firmly in the palm of one hand and carefully insert a skewer in one end and poke it all the way through. Repeat with the remaining balls. Wash and dry your hands and drizzle a little vegetable oil into them, spreading it all over. Take each kebab and gently roll it in your palms to give it a light coating of oil. At this point you can leave the kebabs to marinate for up to 24 hours in the fridge or you can cook straightaway.

To cook, heat a barbecue or griddle pan until hot. Gently lay the kebabs on the grill and cook for 3–4 minutes on one side. Once a golden crust has formed you should be able to turn them over using a fish slice. If they are sticking to the grill, leave them for another minute before trying again. Cook on the other side for a further 3–4 minutes until cooked through.

To make the mint raita, place all the ingredients in a food processor and whizz to a smooth sauce, or use a stick blender to whizz the ingredients in a deep jug. Season to taste with salt and pepper.

Serve the kebabs in warm naan bread, drizzled with a little of the raita, and with a couple of lemon wedges on the side to squeeze over.

For westerners, these Pakistani kebabs are unusual in that the mince is cooked before being shaped into patties. The trick to ensuring they hold their shape is to make sure the mince mixture is cooked until it is completely dry before puréeing and shaping. These can be made with minced lamb or beef, depending on your personal preference.

Note: you will need to begin this recipe the day before you want to eat, as the chana dal needs to soak overnight.

SHAMI BUN KEBAB WITH CORIANDER CHUTNEY

MAKES 4 KEBABS

120g chana dal
2 teaspoons cumin seeds
5 cloves
½–1 teaspoon dried red chilli flakes, to taste
1 tablespoon vegetable oil, plus extra for frying
1 onion, finely chopped
2 garlic cloves, crushed
3cm piece fresh root ginger, grated
300g minced lamb or beef
5 eggs
2 tablespoons gram flour
4 burger buns, split and toasted
salt and freshly ground black pepper
a few red onion, tomato and cucumber slices, to serve

for the coriander chutney
4 tablespoons thick natural yogurt
2 green chillies, roughly chopped
a small bunch of coriander, roughly chopped
a small bunch of mint, leaves roughly chopped
1 garlic clove, crushed

Soak the chana dal overnight in plenty of cold water.

Place the cumin seeds, cloves and red chilli into a large frying pan and set over a medium heat to toast for a minute. Tip into a spice mill or pestle and mortar and grind to a powder. Set aside.

Add 1 tablespoon oil to the frying pan along with the onion and fry over a medium-low heat for 10 minutes until starting to soften. Stir through the garlic, ginger and the ground spices and fry for a further minute. Drain the chana dal and add to the pan along with the mince. Fry for a few minutes, stirring to break up the mince, then pour over 350ml water. Season with salt and pepper, cover loosely with a lid and simmer until the meat and chana dal are tender, about 20 minutes. Remove the lid and continue cooking until the mixture is really dry and starting to catch on the bottom. Stir regularly to prevent it from sticking. Remove from the heat and leave to cool.

Make the chutney by adding all the ingredients to a jug and whizzing with a stick blender. Season to taste with salt and pepper and chill in the fridge until needed.

Once the meat and dal mixture is cool, place in a food processor and whizz to a paste. Add 1 egg and the gram flour and pulse to combine. The mixture should be stiff enough to hold its shape. If it's a little wet, add some more flour. Shape into 4 burgers, place on a plate and cover with cling film, then leave to chill in the fridge for an hour.

When you are ready to cook, add a good glug of oil to a frying pan and set over a medium-high heat. When it's shimmering hot, add the burgers, frying until crisp, about 4–5 minutes on each side. Keep warm on a plate in a low oven (around 110°C/90°C Fan/Gas Mark ¼).

Crack the remaining 4 eggs into the pan and fry them until cooked to your liking. Set 1 egg on top of each burger and keep warm. Assemble the burgers by adding a little onion, tomato and cucumber to the base of each toasted bun, top with a burger and egg, and finally add a dollop of chutney before covering with the top of the bun. Eat immediately.

These delicately spiced Indian samosas are made with proper samosa pastry. It's surprisingly simple to make, and the best thing is that you can add extra flavours, in this case a generous sprinkle of spicy black onion or kalonji seeds. These are fabulous with a dollop of mango pickle or *brinjal* (aubergine pickle) alongside, or with the mint raita on page 174.

SPICED VEGETABLE SAMOSAS

MAKES 16 SAMOSAS

350g potatoes, peeled and cut into 1cm cubes
1 tablespoon vegetable oil, plus extra for greasing
1 small onion, finely chopped
25g piece fresh root ginger, grated
2 garlic cloves, crushed
1 heaped teaspoon garam masala (for homemade see page 160 or use the pav masala on page 182)
100g frozen peas (no need to defrost)
juice of ½ lemon
salt and freshly ground black pepper

for the pastry
250g strong white bread flour
1 tablespoon black onion (kalonji or nigella) seeds
½ teaspoon fine salt
8 tablespoons vegetable oil, plus more for kneading

Make the pastry by stirring the flour, black onion seeds and salt together in a large bowl. Drizzle in the oil and use your fingers and thumbs to rub the oil and flour together, as though you were making a crumble or pastry. Add just enough cold water to mix to a stiff dough – around 6–8 tablespoons – then turn on to a lightly oiled worktop. Knead for 5 minutes until soft, smooth and pliable, then wrap in cling film and set aside to rest while you make the filling.

Add the potatoes to a saucepan and cover generously with boiling water. Set over a medium-high heat and cook until tender, about 15 minutes. Drain well.

Set a frying pan over a medium-low heat and add the oil and onion, frying until translucent and starting to soften, about 10 minutes. Stir through the ginger, garlic and garam masala, or Pav Masala, and season well with salt and pepper. Cook for a further 5 minutes before removing from the heat and stirring through the peas and lemon juice. Set aside to cool (spreading the filling out over a large cold plate will speed this up considerably).

Divide the dough into 16 even balls. The best way to keep them the same size is to divide the dough in half, then each piece in half again, then half again, and then half again. Take one ball and roll out on a lightly oiled worktop until it is a circle of about 12cm in diameter. Lay the circle in the middle of your palm and fold a generous pleat into one side to give you a cone shape, cupping your palm slightly to support it. Add a generous teaspoon of cooled filling into the base of the cone and flatten and pinch the edges to seal up. Depending on how soft your dough is you may need to stick the edges with a dab of cold water. You should be left with a wide triangular samosa with a curved base – don't worry if it looks a touch rustic, it proves you are using homemade dough rather than cheaty filo! Repeat with the remaining balls of dough and the rest of the filling.

Heat the oil in a deep fat fryer to 170°C/340°F and fry the samosas in batches for 7–8 minutes until crisp and golden. Drain on kitchen paper for a few moments before tucking in.

There are two cuisines that could convince me to vegetarian – Italian and Indian, and this recipe is a perfect example of why I have listed Indian as one of the two. Delicious, simple to prepare with ingredients you most likely have in your fridge and storecupboard and wonderfully evocative of Indian street food. Try different vegetables, different ratios of spices and various heat levels. And always double up on hte mint and coriander chutney - ther just never seems to be enough to go around!

PAKORAS WITH MINT AND CORIANDER CHUTNEY

 **Dhruv Baker**
MasterChef UK, 2010 Champion

SERVES 4

200g gram flour
50g self-raising flour
1 teaspoon garam masala
½ teaspoon ground coriander
½ teaspoon ground cumin
1 teaspoon ground turmeric
½ teaspoon ajwain seeds (use cumin seeds if you haven't any ajwain)
1 teaspoon fennel seeds
¼ teaspoon chilli powder
½ teaspoon salt
1 fresh green chilli, finely chopped
1 teaspoon grated ginger
½ teaspoon crushed garlic
250ml water
1 small bunch coriander, finely chopped
1 onion, very finely sliced
2 medium potatoes, grated with a coarse grater
½ small head of cauliflower, cut into little florets
1 teaspoon chaat masala
1 lime
Maldon sea salt, to taste

for the chutney
1 small bunch fresh coriander
3–4 tablespoons mint leaves
1 teaspoon runny honey or caster sugar
juice of 1 lime
50ml water
1 garlic clove, peeled
½ green chilli
50ml thick Greek yogurt
salt and freshly ground black pepper, to taste

To make the chutney, place all the ingredients except the yogurt in a blender. Blend until smooth, then stir through the yogurt and season to taste. Set aside.

Place the flours, spices, salt, fresh chilli, ginger and garlic in a large bowl and combine thoroughly. Add the water, little by little, until you have a lovely thick batter (you may need more or less water than 250ml). Stir through half the chopped coriander, the sliced onion, grated potato and cauliflower florets.

Heat the oil in a deep fat fryer to 170–180°C (325–350°F) (test the temperature by adding a teaspoon of the mixture – when the mixture bubbles, floats and turns golden brown in 45–60 seconds, you are good to go). Drop tablespoon-sized amounts of the mixture into the oil and fry for 2–3 minutes until golden brown and cooked all the way through. Remove with a slotted spoon and drain on kitchen paper.

Season with the chaat masala, a squeeze of lime juice and the Maldon salt, and scatter with the remaining chopped fresh coriander.

Serve the piping hot *pakoras* with the chutney alongside.

Said to have originated as a cheap fast food for the mill workers of Mumbai in the mid-nineteenth century, this simply translates as 'bread' (*pav*, a soft white roll) and 'mashed vegetables' (*bhaji*). However, the generous quantity of butter, along with the exquisite spice blend, elevates this dish beyond the humble. The spice blend makes double the quantity needed for the recipe; store it in an airtight container for 3–4 weeks and use in place of garam masala.

PAV BHAJI

SERVES 4–6

400g potatoes, peeled and cut into 1cm cubes
400g butternut squash, peeled and cut into 1cm cubes
1 tablespoon cumin seeds
75g unsalted butter
1 medium red onion, finely chopped, plus an extra ½ red onion, thinly sliced, to garnish
2 green chillies, chopped
25g piece fresh root ginger, grated
3 garlic cloves, crushed
400g tomatoes, finely chopped
6 soft white rolls, sliced and generously buttered
salt
chopped coriander, to garnish
lemon wedges, to serve

for the pav masala spice blend
5 dried Kashmiri chillies
4 tablespoons coriander seeds
2 tablespoons cumin seeds
1 tablespoon black peppercorns
1 tablespoon fennel seeds
8 cloves
2 black cardamom pods
1 tablespoon amchur (dry mango) powder

Make the spice blend by placing all the ingredients except the amchur powder in a dry frying pan. Set over a medium heat and toast for a minute or two, until a deep, toasty aroma rises from the pan. Tip into a spice mill or pestle and mortar and grind to a powder, then transfer to a bowl and stir through the amchur powder while the spices are still warm. Set aside.

Add the potato and squash cubes to a saucepan and cover generously with boiling water. Set over a high heat, bring back to the boil and cook until tender, around 15 minutes. Drain well and set aside.

Place the cumin seeds in a saucepan and set over a medium heat to toast for a minute. Once you can smell their aroma wafting up from the pan, add the butter and allow it to sizzle and melt before tipping in the chopped red onion and stirring regularly for 10 minutes. Stir through the chilli, ginger and garlic and fry for a further 5 minutes before adding the tomatoes and 3 tablespoons *pav masala* spice mix. Fry for another 5 minutes until thick and fragrant, then add the cooked potato and squash along with 350ml water. Simmer steadily for 20 minutes until thick and rich, mashing with a potato masher as it cooks. Season to taste with salt.

Heat a large frying pan until hot and toast the rolls, butter side down, until crisp.

Spoon the *bhaji* into bowls, scatter over the red onion slices and coriander and serve with a wedge of lemon to squeeze over and a roll to dunk in and scoop it up.

A great Indian snack that goes down a treat with a cold beer – these paneer cheese-stuffed chillies are dipped in a gram (chickpea) flour batter that gives a fabulous nutty flavour. This is a recipe that is very easily doubled or even tripled to feed a party crowd. To get ahead, stuff the chillies and chill in the fridge for up to 3 days, then make up the batter and fry just before serving.

MIRCHI BHAJI

MAKES 12 BHAJIS, SERVING 4–6

60g tamarind
100ml boiling water
2 teaspoons cumin seeds
12 long green chillies
2 tablespoons gram flour
150g paneer, crumbled
salt and freshly ground black
    pepper

for the batter
100g gram flour
50g rice flour
½ teaspoon baking powder
½ teaspoon chilli powder
½ teaspoon fine salt
around 100ml ice-cold water

Place the tamarind in the boiling water, breaking it up with a fork to make a thick, chunky paste, and leave to soak for 30 minutes. Set a small frying pan over a medium heat and add the cumin seeds, toasting for a minute until you can smell their aroma wafting up from the pan. Tip into a small bowl and set aside.

Prepare the chillies by cutting a slit from near the stem to near the tip; you want to create a slit big enough to get the filling inside, but leave the chilli whole rather than separated into two halves. Carefully scrape out the seeds and membranes.

Once the tamarind has soaked, strain the purée through a sieve into the bowl with the toasted cumin, discarding the pips and fibres. Add the gram flour, season well with salt and pepper and stir to a paste. Gently stir through the crumbled paneer, trying not to break it up too much. Take teaspoons of the mixture and use it to stuff the chillies, pressing all the way down to the tip. (The amount of filling here is about right for 12 'regular'-sized long green chillies, but as chillies do vary a lot in size you may find you can stuff a few more or a few less than 12.)

Make the batter by adding the gram and rice flours to a large bowl and stirring through the baking powder, chilli powder and salt. Pour in the ice-cold water, whisking constantly until you have a smooth batter. It should be thick enough to coat the chillies evenly (test it by dipping a clean finger into the batter; it should have a nice even coating). If it's too thick, add a splash more water; if it's too thin and runs off, add a sprinkle more gram flour.

Heat the oil in a deep fat fryer to 180°C/350°F. When it's hot, dip a few chillies into the batter and place them straight into the fryer. Work in batches of 3 or 4 so you don't overload the fryer and cool the oil. Fry for about 5 minutes until crisp and golden. Drain over kitchen paper and repeat with the other chillies. Serve immediately and eat while still hot.

Aloo tikki are a classic Indian *chaat*, or 'snack food', typically served from street food carts. Subtly spiced, soft and creamy mashed potatoes are shaped and fried into crisp cakes and topped with a little dollop of cool yogurt and a fiery sweet chutney. They are a triumph of textures and really quite addictive. I've made medium-sized potato cakes that will take you about three generous bites to eat, but you could easily halve the size to make canapés for a party.

ALOO TIKKI WITH DATE AND TAMARIND CHUTNEY

MAKES 12, SERVING 4–6

1kg potatoes, peeled and cut
 into even chunks
1 tablespoon vegetable oil, plus
 extra for frying
2 teaspoons mustard seeds
1 teaspoon cumin seeds
3 spring onions, finely chopped
2 garlic cloves, crushed
1cm piece fresh root ginger,
 finely grated
50g butter
a bunch of coriander, chopped,
 plus extra to serve
2 tablespoons cornflour
salt and freshly ground black
 pepper
4 tablespoons thick natural
 yogurt, to serve

**for the date and tamarind
chutney**
100g pitted dates, roughly
 chopped
225ml boiling water
60g tamarind
1–2 teaspoons dried red chilli
 flakes, to taste
1 teaspoon cumin seeds
a pinch of salt

Add the potatoes to a pan of lightly salted water and bring to the boil. Cook until just tender, about 15–20 minutes.

Meanwhile, add the oil to a frying pan and set over a medium heat. When it's hot, add the mustard and cumin seeds and allow to fry for a minute or so. When the mustard seeds start to pop, add the spring onions, garlic and ginger, and season with salt and pepper, stir frying for a few minutes until the spring onions start to soften. Remove from the heat and set aside.

Drain the potatoes well and tip back into the pan, allowing the steam to rise for a couple of minutes to make sure they are really dry. Mash well until smooth, then add the butter and beat until combined. Leave to cool for 10 minutes before stirring through the spring onion mixture, coriander and cornflour.

Take heaped tablespoons of the mixture and shape into balls with your hands, flattening each into a little burger shape. Lay on a plate and leave to go cold, then chill in the fridge for an hour – this really helps to get a lovely crisp outer shell on the *aloo tikki* when you fry them, so don't be tempted to skip this step.

While they are chilling, make the date and tamarind chutney. Tip the dates into a small saucepan and pour over 125ml boiling water. Set aside to soak for 30 minutes. Add the tamarind to a jug and pour over the remaining boiling water, breaking up the flesh with a fork and mixing to form a lumpy paste. Set aside for 30 minutes. Add the chilli and cumin to a small frying pan and toast for a couple of minutes. Tip into a spice mill or pestle and mortar and grind to a powder. Set aside.

Once both the dates and tamarind have finished soaking, hang a sieve over the saucepan and strain the tamarind on to the dates, discarding the pips and fibres. Cover the pan with a lid and simmer over a low heat for 15 minutes, after which time the dates should be really soft and plump. Whizz to a purée, either in the pan with a stick blender or in a small food processor, then return to the pan. Add the ground spices and the salt and cook over a low heat for 5 minutes, stirring frequently. Scoop into a bowl and allow to go cold.

To cook the *aloo tikki*, add a good glug of oil to a large frying pan and set over a medium-high heat. Once the oil is shimmering hot, carefully add the *aloo tikki*, well spaced out, and allow to fry until really crisp and golden brown, about 4 minutes. Turn over with a fish slice or palette knife and cook for another 3–4 minutes or so.

To serve, dollop a teaspoon of yogurt on top of each *aloo tikki*, and top that with a little of the chutney. Finally, sprinkle over a little coriander and eat while still hot and crisp.

Softly set scrambled eggs loaded with vegetables, spices and herbs make a spectacular and unusual brunch dish. Traditionally eaten without cutlery, and using torn off bits of bread to scoop up the egg, this is a very popular street breakfast in India to fuel the workers.

EGG BHURJI WITH BUTTERY PARATHAS

SERVES 4–6

1 tablespoon cumin seeds
50g butter
2 red onions, finely chopped
3cm piece fresh root ginger, grated
2 garlic cloves, chopped
2–3 long green chillies, or to taste, chopped
1 teaspoon ground turmeric
½–1 teaspoon chilli powder, or to taste
200g frozen peas (no need to defrost)
4 large vine tomatoes, chopped
12 eggs, lightly whisked
a bunch of coriander, chopped
salt and freshly ground black pepper

for the parathas
250g wholemeal bread flour
250g strong white bread flour
1 tablespoon black onion (kalonji or nigella) seeds
½ teaspoon caster sugar
½ teaspoon fine salt
300ml warm water\vegetable oil, for greasing
50g ghee or softened butter

To make the parathas, add the flours, bllack onion seeds, sugar and salt to a large bowl and stir together. Pour in the water, mixing with a knife to a crumbly dough. Lightly oil the worktop and tip the dough on to it. Knead for 5 minutes until smooth, soft and elastic. Set aside to rest for 15 minutes.

Re-oil the worktop and roll out the dough into a large rectangle, around 35 x 45cm and 5mm thick. Spread the dough all over with the ghee or softened butter then roll up tightly like a Swiss roll. Chop into 12 even-sized pieces. Take one piece and turn it on to a cut end, pressing down firmly to form a disc, then roll the disc out to a rough circle around 17–18cm and 2mm thick. Repeat with the remaining pieces.

Set a large frying pan over a medium-high heat. Once hot, add one of the parathas and cook for a couple of minutes, pressing the surface with a fish slice from time to time to ensure it cooks evenly. Flip over and cook the other side for a further couple of minutes. Transfer to a plate and keep warm in a low oven (around 110°C/90°C Fan/Gas Mark ¼), loosely covered in foil, while you cook the remaining parathas.

While the parathas are keeping warm, you can begin the eggs. Set a heavy-based saucepan over a medium heat and add the cumin seeds. Allow to toast for a couple of minutes before reducing the heat a little and adding the butter. Once the butter has melted, add the onion and cook, stirring occasionally, for 15 minutes or so, until soft and very lightly coloured.

Stir through the ginger, garlic, chilli, turmeric, chilli powder, peas and tomatoes and fry for another couple of minutes. Tip in the eggs, season with salt and pepper and stir briefly to mix. Leave the eggs to set for a couple of minutes before giving them another brief stir; repeat this process until the eggs are softly set. It's lovely to keep the textures of the soft egg and vegetables a little distinct from each other, and if you stir too often or too vigorously it all becomes a bit mushed up.

Fold through the coriander just before serving. Serve the egg as soon as it has set, with the warm parathas to scoop it up.

Chaat is the term for 'snack' in India, and *papdi* are delectable little fried pieces of dough. Pretty as a picture and an absolute explosion of taste and texture, this is one of my favourite Indian street foods – a sort of Indian version of nachos! You can line up all the elements in dishes well ahead of time, then assemble at the last minute so the *papdi* stay crisp.

PAPDI CHAAT

SERVES 4–6

for the papdi
150g plain flour
150g plain wholemeal flour
1 teaspoon cumin seeds
1 teaspoon ajwain seeds
½ teaspoon fine salt
50g ghee or softened butter

for the crunchy chickpeas
1 x 400g can chickpeas, drained
    and rinsed
1 tablespoon vegetable oil
1 teaspoon coriander seeds,
    roughly ground
1 teaspoon cumin seeds,
    roughly ground
1 teaspoon red chilli flakes
sea salt flakes
freshly ground black pepper

for the roast aubergine
1 aubergine, cut into 1cm cubes
    (about 350g)
2 tablespoons vegetable oil
2 teaspoons black onion (kalonji
    or nigella) seeds
½ teaspoon ground turmeric
salt and freshly ground black
    pepper

for the chaat masala
1 tablespoon cumin seeds
1 teaspoon black peppercorns
1 tablespoon amchur (dry
    mango) powder
½ teaspoon salt

to serve
4–6 vine tomatoes, chopped
    (about 300g)
1 red onion, finely chopped
6 tablespoons thick natural
    yogurt
1 quantity of date and tamarind
    chutney (see page 188)
1 quantity of coriander chutney
    (see page 197)

For the *papdi*, stir together the flours, cumin and ajwain seeds with the salt. Add the ghee or butter and just enough water to bring it together to a firm dough – around 8 tablespoons. Tip on to the worktop and knead for a couple of minutes, then put back into the bowl, cover and leave to rest for 30 minutes.

Preheat the oven to 200°C/180°C Fan/Gas Mark 6. Tip the chickpeas into the centre of a clean tea towel, bring up the sides and dry the chickpeas thoroughly by pressing gently all over. Tip into a bowl and stir through the oil, coriander, cumin and chilli. Season with salt and pepper and stir well to coat. Spread out in a single layer on a baking tray.

Place the aubergine in the same bowl (no need to wash it) and add the vegetable oil, black onion seeds and turmeric. Season with salt and pepper and mix thoroughly. Spread out in a thin layer on another baking tray. Put both chickpeas and aubergine into the hot oven and roast for 25–30 minutes, turning halfway through. The aubergine should be soft and tender, the chickpeas crisp and crunchy. Set both aside to cool.

While they are cooking, make the chutneys, using the recipes on pages 188 and 197. Add a splash more water to the date and tamarind chutney to make it easier to drizzle, and whizz up the coriander chutney until it's a little paler in colour.

Once the *papdi* dough has rested, roll it out on a lightly floured worktop to a thickness of about 2mm. Prick all over with a fork to stop it from puffing up too much on cooking, then cut the dough into squares of about 4cm. Heat the oil in a deep fat fryer to 180°C/350°F and fry in 2 or 3 batches for about 3 minutes until crisp and golden. Drain over kitchen paper and set aside.

To make the *chaat masala*, toast the cumin seeds for a minute or two in a dry frying pan set over a medium heat. Once you can smell their aroma wafting from the pan, tip into a spice mill or pestle and mortar, add the peppercorns and grind to a powder. Add the amchur powder and salt and mix together for a few seconds to combine. Tip into a bowl.

To serve, place a layer of *papdi* over a large platter for sharing or a few smaller plates. Scatter over some tomato and red onion and top with a little roast aubergine. Add a few dollops of yogurt and chutneys, scatter over the crunchy chickpeas and finish with a sprinkling of *chaat masala*. Serve immediately.

Kati means 'stick' or 'skewer' in Bengali, and this street snack, originating from Kolkata in northern India, consists of a deliciously spiced beef kebab, rolled in a double wrap of paratha bread and a thin omelette.

KATI ROLLS

MAKES 4 ROLLS

500g beef skirt
juice of 1 lime
1 tablespoon vegetable oil
2 garlic cloves, crushed
1 teaspoon ground turmeric
1 teaspoon fenugreek seeds
½ teaspoon black peppercorns
4 cloves
8 eggs
½ small red onion, thinly sliced
salt and freshly ground black
    pepper

for the parathas
300g brown chapati flour, or a
    50:50 blend of wholemeal and
    white bread flours
1 teaspoon cumin seeds
1 teaspoon salt
1 tablespoon vegetable oil, plus
    extra for greasing and frying

for the coriander chutney
2 bunches of coriander (about
    50g), stalks and leaves roughly
    chopped
1 green chilli, roughly chopped
juice of 1 lime
1 garlic clove, chopped
1 teaspoon sugar, or to taste

you will need
4 metal or bamboo skewers (if
    using bamboo, soak in cold
    water for an hour before
    using to prevent them from
    burning)

Slice the beef into 1cm-thick strips across the grain and add to a large bowl with the lime juice, oil, garlic and turmeric. Grind the fenugreek, black peppercorns and cloves to a fine powder in a spice mill or pestle and mortar, then add to the beef. Mix together so each piece of beef is well coated, cover with cling film and set aside at room temperature for an hour or so; or if you want to make it ahead of time, you can leave it in the fridge overnight. Once marinated, thread the strips of beef on to the skewers.

To make the parathas, mix the flour, cumin and salt together in a bowl, then add 175ml water and the oil, stirring with a tablespoon to form a stiff dough. Tip on to a lightly oiled worktop and knead for 5 minutes until smooth and elastic. Divide into 4 even pieces then roll each into a long, thin snake around 70cm long and about the thickness of your little finger. Starting at one end, coil it up like a snail shell, then use a rolling pin to roll it out into a large, flat disc of about 25cm in diameter and 2mm thick, trying to keep the shape as circular as possible by rotating it regularly. If it starts to stick, add a little more oil.

For the coriander chutney, add all the ingredients to a deep jug and whizz up with a stick blender, adding a tablespoon or two of cold water, just enough to make a paste. Season to taste and set aside.

To cook the parathas, take a large frying pan and set it over a high heat. Once hot, add a drizzle of oil, spreading it over the base of the pan with a scrunched-up bit of kitchen paper. Lay in one paratha and let it cook for a minute or two on just one side until brown and slightly puffed up. Transfer to a plate and repeat with the remaining parathas.

Reduce the heat to medium and add a little more oil. Crack 2 eggs into a bowl and whisk together with a little salt and pepper, then pour into the pan, swirling about to make a large, flat omelette about the same size as the parathas. Once it has set on the bottom but is still sticky on the surface, place a paratha, cooked side down, on to the egg, pressing together firmly, then flip the whole lot over so the uncooked bread faces down. Let it cook for another minute then transfer to a plate and keep warm in a low oven (around 110°C/90°C Fan/Gas Mark ¼) while you repeat with the remaining eggs and parathas.

To cook the beef, heat a griddle pan or barbecue until really hot and sear the kebabs over a high heat until they are cooked to your liking. I like mine crisp on the outside but still a touch pink inside.

To serve, take one of the parathas and spread a generous tablespoon of chutney on to the omelette side. Use a fork to pull the beef off a skewer into the middle and sprinkle over a little sliced onion before rolling up tight. Eat while still hot, wrapping greaseproof paper around the bottom of the roll to make it easier to eat.

A rice and lentil pancake stuffed with a spicy potato filling, the *masala dosa* is a fabulous vegetarian street food dish from India. The rice and lentils for the batter have a long soaking and fermenting time, and the fermenting process can be somewhat unpredictable, especially in colder climes. So give yourself plenty of time for this recipe. If the batter has not risen after 12–15 hours at room temperature, it is acceptable to help it along with some yeast.

Note: you will need to begin this recipe the day before you want to eat, as the rice and lentils need to soak, then ferment overnight.

MASALA DOSA

MAKES 8–10 DOSAS

800g potatoes, peeled and cut into 2cm cubes
3 tablespoons vegetable oil
2 teaspoons mustard seeds
10 curry leaves
2 onions, chopped
3–4 hot green chillies, sliced
3 garlic cloves, crushed
3cm piece fresh root ginger, grated
½ teaspoon ground turmeric
50g butter (optional)
salt and freshly ground black pepper
chopped coriander, to garnish
chutney, e.g. ready made mango chutney, or coriander chutney (see page 197), date and tamarind chutney (see page 188) or coriander coconut chutney (see page 206), to serve

for the dosa batter
400g easy-cook (parboiled) basmati rice
200g urid dal (split black lentils)
70g chana dal
1 teaspoon fenugreek seeds
2 tablespoons chopped coriander
1 teaspoon salt
½ teaspoon fast-action yeast (optional)
2 tablespoons warm water (optional)
vegetable oil, for frying

For the *dosa* batter, add the rice, urid dal, chana dal and fenugreek seeds to a bowl and cover with warm water. Leave to soak for 6–8 hours. Do not drain or rinse – you will wash away the wild yeasts and reduce your chances of a successful fermentation. Working in batches, grind the rice and pulses with enough of the soaking water to make a smooth, creamy batter. A high-powered smoothie maker is perfect as it will grind the batter really well, but a liquidiser or powerful food processor would also work. Pour the batches of batter into a large bowl and stir through the coriander and salt. Cover with cling film and leave at room temperature overnight. By the morning, the *dosa* batter should have risen and be bubbly on the surface. If nothing has happened, mix the yeast with the 2 tablespoons of warm water, then stir through the batter and leave for a further 1–2 hours at room temperature.

Alternatively, if there are promising signs of fermentation on first checking, leave for a few hours longer without adding yeast. If it's brilliantly bubbly (well done!) you can now transfer the bowl to the fridge to halt fermentation until you are ready to cook – it will keep in the fridge for a few days. At this stage you may need to thin out the batter by whisking through a little cold water – it needs to be thick enough to coat the back of a spoon nicely, but thin enough to spread out to a pancake; the consistency of thick double cream is about right.

To make the filling, add the potatoes to a pan of lightly salted boiling water and cook for 12–15 minutes until tender. Drain well and set aside.

Add the oil to a generous frying pan with the mustard seeds and curry leaves and set over a medium-high heat. Once the mustard seeds start to pop, stir through the onions and chillies and reduce the heat to a minimum. Allow the onions to cook slowly to a soft melting mass, stirring occasionally, for about 40 minutes. Stir through the garlic, ginger and turmeric and season with salt and pepper, frying for another couple of minutes. Tip in the cooked potatoes and add the butter, if using, to add richness. Stir well over a low heat for a few minutes, mashing the potato a little as you go. Keep the filling warm while you make the *dosas*.

Take a large frying pan and add a little oil. Set over a medium-high heat. Once the oil is hot, brush it all over the surface of the pan using a piece of scrunched-up kitchen paper. Pour a ladleful of batter into the centre and, using the underside of the ladle, quickly swirl it around to spread out the batter to a thin layer. Allow to cook for a minute or two, then test if it's ready to turn by lifting an edge with a fish slice. It should be golden and crisp. Flip over carefully and cook the other side. Spoon a little potato filling on to one side and fold the other side over the top. Serve immediately while you make the rest of the *dosas*, or keep warm in a low oven (around 110°C/90°C Fan/Gas Mark ¼).

Garnish with a little coriander and serve with the chutney of your choice.

There are many theories about how this dish gets its great name, one of which suggests it was invented in 1965, another that it originally contained 65 types of chilli. Either way, it's a deliciously fiery Indian snack that's great with a cold beer.

Note: you will need to begin this recipe several hours before you want to eat, or ideally the day before, as the chicken needs time to marinate.

CHICKEN 65

SERVES 4 AS A SNACK

1 tablespoon cumin seeds
1 tablespoon coriander seeds
500g skinless chicken thigh fillets, cut into bite-sized pieces
4 tablespoons natural yogurt
3 teaspoons rice flour
2 teaspoons red wine vinegar
3cm piece fresh root ginger, grated
3 garlic cloves, crushed
2 teaspoons paprika
1 teaspoon chilli flakes, or to taste
½ teaspoon ground turmeric
1 teaspoon vegetable oil
a handful of curry leaves
2 red chillies, thinly sliced
salt and freshly ground black pepper
½ red onion, thinly sliced, to serve
chopped coriander, to serve
lemon wedges (optional), to serve

Set a small pan over a medium heat and add the cumin and coriander seeds. Toast for a minute or two until you can smell their aroma wafting up from the pan, then tip into a spice mill or pestle and mortar and grind to a powder. Transfer into a large bowl.

Add the chicken to the bowl, along with the yogurt, rice flour, vinegar, ginger, garlic, paprika, chilli flakes, turmeric and a little black pepper, stirring well to mix. Cover and leave to marinate in the fridge for at least 2 hours, or ideally overnight if you have time.

When you are ready to cook, preheat the oil in a deep fat fryer to 180°C/350°F. Add about 6–8 chicken pieces and fry for 4 minutes until golden and cooked through. Transfer to a plate lined with kitchen paper and repeat until you have cooked all the chicken.

Add the oil to a wok or large frying pan and set over a high heat. When it's hot, tip in the cooked chicken, the curry leaves and red chilli, season with salt and pepper and stir fry for 2–3 minutes until the curry leaves have wilted and everything is hot and crisp.

Tip into a serving dish, scatter with the red onion and coriander and serve immediately with lemon wedges to squeeze over.

The creamiest, most fragrant lollies ever, kulfi are made by evaporating whole milk until it's rich and almost caramelised. The beauty of enriching the milk like this is that you don't need an ice cream maker to churn and break up the ice crystals; passing this mixture through a fine sieve ensures a velvety texture. Traditionally in India these are made in conical metal kulfi moulds, but I have used a 12-hole lolly mould; dariole moulds or ramekins would also work.

MANGO AND CARDAMOM KULFI LOLLIES

MAKES ABOUT 6–12 LOLLIES, DEPENDING ON THE SIZE AND SHAPE OF YOUR MOULDS

1 litre whole milk
8 green cardamom pods, bruised until open
1 x 400g can condensed milk
2 large ripe mangoes
1 teaspoon vegetable oil
3 tablespoons shelled unsalted pistachio nuts

you will need
lolly moulds and wooden lolly sticks

Pour the milk into the largest saucepan you have; a stockpot or jam pan is ideal. Add the cardamom pods and bring to the boil over a high heat, then reduce to a medium heat and simmer rapidly for 30 minutes, stirring regularly until the milk has reduced by three-quarters. Stir very frequently towards the end of simmering to prevent the milk from burning. You are looking for the milk to reduce to about 250ml – it will be quite thick and almost granular in texture.

Remove from the heat and strain through a fine sieve into a bowl, using the back of a wooden spoon to push as much through as possible. Discard the cardamom pods.

Add the condensed milk to the reduced milk and stir until thoroughly combined. Set aside to cool.

Peel and chop the mango flesh, adding it to a blender or liquidiser along with any juice. Purée until smooth, then strain through a fine sieve into the milk mixture, discarding any mango fibre.

Lightly oil the lolly moulds using a scrunched-up piece of kitchen paper to spread a thin, even layer all over the insides. Pour the kulfi mixture into the moulds and transfer to the freezer. Freeze for about an hour or so until the mixture is firm enough for the lolly sticks to stand up straight. Insert the lolly sticks, then freeze again until solid.

Add the pistachios to a small frying pan and toast over a medium-high heat for a couple of minutes. Tip on to a chopping board and chop roughly.

Remove the kulfi from the freezer and allow to warm at room temperature for 30 minutes before removing from the moulds, sliding a table knife around the inside to help ease them out. Roll them in the chopped pistachios and serve.

A fabulously unusual Sri Lankan brunch dish, egg hoppers are coconut and rice flour pancakes cooked with a steamed egg in the middle. Traditionally cooked in a 'hopper pan' – a small high-sided wok – that gives the pancakes a classic bowl shape, but a non-stick wok or frying pan is fine.

Note: you will need to begin this recipe at least 6 hours before you want to eat, to allow the batter time to ferment and rise at room temperature; ideally, whisk it up the night before and leave in the fridge overnight to prove slowly.

EGG HOPPERS WITH CORIANDER COCONUT CHUTNEY

MAKES 6 EGG HOPPERS

100g creamed coconut, grated
600ml boiling water
200g rice flour
1 teaspoon fast-action yeast
½ teaspoon caster sugar
vegetable oil, for frying
6 large eggs

for the coriander coconut chutney
2 generous bunches of
    coriander, leaves and stalks
    roughly chopped
a handful of mint leaves
200g coconut flesh, fresh or
    frozen, grated
juice of 2 limes
2 or 3 green chillies, roughly
    chopped
2 garlic cloves, roughly chopped
2 teaspoons sugar
salt and freshly ground black
    pepper, to taste

Add the grated creamed coconut to a large bowl and pour over the boiling water, stirring well until it has dissolved. Set aside for 10–15 minutes until the bowl is just warm to the touch – if it's too hot it will kill the yeast.

Sprinkle over the flour, yeast and sugar and whisk until smooth. Cover and set aside for at least 6 hours at room temperature or overnight in the fridge.

For the coriander coconut chutney, add all the ingredients to a deep jug and whizz until smooth with a stick blender. Set aside for the flavours to mingle.

When the pancake batter is ready, give it a good whisk to mix through. Drizzle a little oil into a small non-stick frying pan or wok and set over a high heat, spreading the oil into an even layer using a scrunched-up bit of kitchen paper. When it is smoking hot, pour in a generous ladleful of batter, swirling it around quickly up the sides. Crack an egg in the centre, reduce the heat a little and cover with a lid or piece of kitchen foil. Cook for 3 minutes or so until the egg is cooked to your liking.

Use a table knife or palette knife to ease the egg hopper from the pan to a plate and repeat with the remaining batter and eggs. Spoon the chutney over the hoppers and serve.

With the texture and nuttiness of a falafel and the added succulence of king prawns, these Sri Lankan shrimp *vadai* (prawn fritters) are hugely moreish. The *pol sambol* is a fiery coconut-based dry chutney that goes well with many spicy dishes – try it with the egg hoppers on page 206. Maldive fish flakes are hard to source, but do use them in place of the fish sauce if you can find them.

SHRIMP VADAI WITH POL SAMBOL

MAKES ABOUT 16–18 VADAI, SERVING 4–6 AS A SNACK

200g chana dal
1 red onion, roughly chopped
1 small bunch of coriander, roughly chopped
3 or 4 green chillies, to taste
2 garlic cloves, roughly chopped
25g piece fresh root ginger, grated
1 teaspoon ground turmeric
250g raw prawns, peeled and roughly chopped
salt and freshly ground black pepper

for the pol sambol
200g fresh grated coconut, or 150g desiccated coconut soaked in 50ml boiling water for 30 minutes
1 red onion, grated
2 garlic cloves, crushed
juice of 2 limes
3–5 teaspoons dried red chilli powder, to taste
1 teaspoon fish sauce, or 1 tablespoon Maldive fish flakes
1 teaspoon caster sugar

Soak the chana dal for 2 hours in plenty of cold water, then drain and place in a food processor. Pulse until finely ground, then add the onion, coriander, chillies, garlic, ginger and turmeric. Season well with salt and pepper and process until smooth. Scrape into a bowl and tip in the chopped prawns, mixing them through thoroughly. Take tablespoonfuls of the mixture and shape into balls, flattening slightly into mini patties. Set aside.

To make the *pol sambol*, place the coconut in a large frying pan and set over a medium heat. Toast, stirring frequently, for about 3 minutes until golden in places and aromatic. Remove from the heat into a large bowl. Stir through the onion, garlic, lime juice, chilli powder, fish flakes or sauce, sugar and add a good sprinkle of salt. Taste to check the seasoning: it should be hot, sharp and just a little sweet. Add more chilli, lime juice or sugar, to taste.

Heat the oil in a deep fat fryer to 180°C/350°F. Fry the *vadai* in batches for 3–4 minutes until deep golden brown and crisp. Drain over kitchen paper briefly before serving with the *pol sambol*.

I adore egg curries; if you've never made one and are a touch sceptical, I urge you to give this Sri Lankan version a go. Eggs and spices are simply made for each other, and here you have soft-boiled eggs fried until crisp on the outside, served in a generous puddle of curry sauce – perfect speedy post-pub tucker if you get your sauce ready beforehand. You could also serve this as a full meal with plenty of steamed rice on the side.

TURMERIC FRIED EGGS WITH CURRY SAUCE

SERVES 4 AS A GENEROUS SNACK

1 tablespoon coriander seeds
½ teaspoon cumin seeds
½ teaspoon mustard seeds
½ teaspoon fenugreek seeds
½ teaspoon black peppercorns
1cm piece cinnamon stick
1 bay leaf, torn into pieces
1 tablespoon coconut or
    vegetable oil
1 medium onion, grated
2 garlic cloves, crushed
15g piece fresh root ginger,
    grated
1 or 2 green chillies, finely
    chopped, to taste
½ teaspoon shrimp paste
3 medium tomatoes, sliced in
    half
1 x 400ml can coconut milk
1 teaspoon coconut sugar, or
    brown sugar/palm sugar
8 large eggs
2 teaspoons ground turmeric
1 teaspoon sea salt flakes
vegetable oil for frying
salt and freshly ground black
    pepper
chopped coriander, to garnish
red onion, sliced, to garnish
naan bread, to serve

Take a large saucepan and set it over a medium-high heat. When it's hot, add the coriander, cumin, mustard, fenugreek, black peppercorns, cinnamon stick and bay leaf and toast for a minute. Scoop out the spices into a spice mill or pestle and mortar and grind to a powder. Set aside.

Add the coconut or vegetable oil to the pan along with the onion and stir fry over a medium heat for 10 minutes until soft and translucent. Add the spice powder, garlic, ginger, green chilli and shrimp paste and stir fry for a further 5 minutes.

Starting from the cut side, grate the tomato halves into the pan until you get down to the skin (discard the skin). Stir well to mix, add 250ml water and cook for about 10 minutes, stirring regularly until thick and concentrated. Season to taste, then add the coconut milk and coconut or palm sugar and simmer steadily for about 5 minutes until it reaches a thick double-cream consistency. At this point you can turn off the heat and leave the sauce until you are ready to eat (once cool, store it in the fridge if you are leaving it for more than 2 hours).

When you are ready to eat, put the eggs in a large pan and cover well with cold water. Set over a medium-high heat and bring to the boil. When they start to boil, turn the heat down a little and simmer steadily for 4 minutes. Drain and run under cold water until cool enough to peel. Sprinkle the turmeric and sea salt over a large plate and roll the peeled eggs around until coated.

Pour 1cm of vegetable oil into a wok or large deep frying pan and set over a medium-high heat. When it's hot enough (test it by throwing in a cube of bread; it should brown in 30 seconds), carefully add the eggs one at a time using a long-handled spoon. Fry until crisp and golden, about 4 minutes, turning regularly and spooning a little hot oil over the top as they cook, just like regular fried eggs.

Reheat the sauce and divide between bowls. Top each bowl with an egg or two, sprinkle over some coriander and onion slices and tuck in, scooping up the gravy as you eat the eggs with a little naan bread.

Kottu roti (literally 'chopped roti') is perhaps *the* defining street food of Sri Lanka, their equivalent of a burger in terms of sheer popularity. The curry recipe calls for a lot of ingredients and preparation, so I've made double the quantity you need, so you can freeze a batch for next time. You could also speed things up by using leftover curry and by preparing the veg in advance, so when you are ready to eat it's as quick as a regular stir fry. It's traditionally cooked on a large flat griddle over a barbecue, but a large wok or frying pan is fine too.

CHICKEN CURRY KOTTU ROTI

SERVES 4–6

600g skinless chicken thigh fillets, cut into bite-sized pieces
3 tablespoons vegetable or coconut oil
1 onion, grated
8 garlic cloves, thinly sliced
60g piece fresh root giner: 30g grated, 30g finely sliced
3 medium tomatoes, halved
1 x 400ml can coconut milk
1 tablespoon cider vinegar
1 teaspoon salt
4 large roti bread, or parathas (see page 190) or soft flour tortillas
1 leek, finely sliced
5 spring onions, thinly sliced
1 carrot, cut into matchsticks
200g white cabbage, thinly sliced
3 green chillies, chopped
20 fresh curry leaves
1 tablespoon cumin seeds
2 tablespoons soy sauce
2 eggs, lightly beaten
lime wedges, to serve

Sri Lankan roast spice powder

2 tablespoons coriander seeds
1 tablespoon cumin seeds
1 tablespoon raw basmati rice
2 teaspoons fennel seeds
1 teaspoon fenugreek seeds
1 teaspoon black peppercorns
1 teaspoon mustard seeds
1 teaspoon ground turmeric
6cm piece cinnamon stick
5 cardamom pods, bruised until open
5 cloves
3 dried red Kashmiri chillies
2 sprigs fresh curry leaves, leaves picked

Begin by making the spice powder. Add all the ingredients to a dry frying pan and set over a medium heat. Toast the spices, stirring regularly, for about 3 minutes until they are a deep colour and smell deliciously aromatic. Remove from the heat, tip into a spice mill or pestle and mortar and grind to a powder.

Transfer the spices into a large bowl and add the chicken and a tablespoon of oil, mixing well until the meat is evenly coated. Set aside at room temperature for an hour to marinate, or if you want to make it ahead of time, you can leave it in the fridge overnight.

Pour another tablespoon of oil into a large heavy-based pan and set over a medium-low heat. Add the onion, half the garlic and the grated ginger, and sweat gently for 10 minutes until translucent and softening. Add the chicken, increase the heat a little and stir fry for a few minutes until the meat is sealed. Finally, add the tomato, coconut milk, cider vinegar and ½ teaspoon salt, bring to a simmer and allow to bubble and reduce for 20 minutes, stirring regularly.

Once cooked, leave the curry to go cold. You only use half the curry, so freeze the remainder for another time.

When you are ready to eat, heat a large wok, frying pan or grill plate until really hot and toast the roti one at a time on both sides. When they are all toasted, chop into 3cm pieces and set aside.

Add the remaining tablespoon of oil to the pan or griddle and add the leek, spring onion, carrot and cabbage, stir frying over a high heat for a couple of minutes until just starting to colour. Add the sliced ginger, the remaining garlic, chillies, curry leaves, cumin, soy and ½ teaspoon of salt and stir fry for a further minute. Push the vegetables to one side and add the beaten egg, stirring until just scrambled, then mix through the vegetables.

Add the cooled curry, stirring through until everything is really well mixed. Finally, stir through the chopped roti and cook until everything is piping hot. Serve immediately with lime wedges to squeeze over.

ASIA AND AUSTRALIA

Think of Asian street food and it is perhaps the fragrant delights of South East Asia that come to mind first. Certainly, the evocative, exotic (and sometimes chaotic!) night markets of Bangkok and Singapore are legendary worldwide, and were my first memorable introduction to street eating many years ago. However, this is a vast area of the world, spanning all climates and with rich and varied cultures, and naturally the food follows suit.

There is so much to get excited about in this chapter, from the warming soups of *banmian* and *odeng* broth to the refreshing, and very unusual, tropical rojak salad of Malaysia. Thai and Vietnamese dishes are known throughout the world, famous for their exquisite use of fragrant herbs and spices, but do delve into neighbouring Cambodia's recipes for a different but equally delicious take on South East Asian flavours. MasterChef champions offer some iconic dishes from this region, such as Andy Allen's Thai prawns, Christine Ha's take on a Vietnamese spicy beef soup, Ping Coombes' *chai tau kueh* or Woo Wai Leong's oyster omelette. Or for a more dainty take on that hearty Oz classic, the meat pie, try Brent Owen's nostalgia-inspired recipe. Meanwhile, both Tim Anderson and Adam Liaw offer great recipes from Japan with *daigaku imo* and karaage chicken rolls.

Lastly, don't confine yourselves to eating these recipes at home. Just as in the countries they originate from, many of these recipes are ideal for on-the-move eating: the tea eggs are a stunning-looking treat on a picnic; the Korean egg toast makes a fab breakfast on the go; and the *kimbap* are the perfect use for a few leftovers in a lunch box.

I absolutely love these marbled hard-boiled eggs. Popular with street vendors across China, they are exquisite to look at, taste mighty fine and are a doddle to make. This recipe is very easily adapted to make as many tea eggs as you like: you don't really need to increase the spices and soy, just make sure the eggs are simmering in a single submerged layer. The longer you steep them post-simmering, the more pronounced the marbling and the tastier they get.

Note: you will need to begin this recipe at least 6 hours before you want to eat (the longer the better!), as the eggs need time to steep.

TEA EGGS

MAKES 8 TEA EGGS

8 eggs
150ml soy sauce
2 tablespoons black tea leaves
  (from 2 teabags)
1 tablespoon granulated sugar
4 star anise
1 cinnamon stick, snapped in
  half
1 teaspoon Sichuan peppercorns
1 tangerine, peel only

Put the eggs into a saucepan in a single layer and cover well with cold water. Set over a medium heat and bring to the boil. Reduce the heat to a steady simmer and cook for 6 minutes. Remove from the heat and place under cold running water until they are cool enough to handle.

Take one egg and cup it in the palm of your hand. With a teaspoon in the other hand, use the back of the spoon to gently tap the egg all over to form lots of tiny cracks, keeping the shell on the egg. Repeat with the other eggs.

Return all the eggs to the pan, again in a single layer, and just cover with cold water. Add the soy sauce, tea leaves, sugar, star anise, cinnamon stick, peppercorns and tangerine peel and set back on the hob over a medium heat. Bring to the boil, reduce the heat to a simmer, cover with a lid and cook for 2 hours. Check every once in a while that the eggs are still submerged and top up with a splash more water if necessary.

Remove from the heat and allow to cool in the tea liquor. Once cold, transfer to the fridge and leave infusing for a minimum of 6 hours; they will keep in the fridge for up to 3 days. The longer they steep, the stronger and more salty they will become.

When you are ready to eat, simply peel and munch.

Jiaozi are gorgeous little stuffed dumplings that are either steamed, as in this recipe, or fried until crisp. They are a traditional part of a Chinese New Year feast, but so popular that they are also heartily consumed all year round, be it for breakfast, lunch, dinner or just general snacking. *Jiaozi* freeze really well and can be steamed from frozen.

STEAMED JIAOZI STUFFED WITH PORK AND CABBAGE

MAKES 40 DUMPLINGS, SERVING 4–6

250g plain flour, plus extra for dipping
250g minced pork
150g Savoy cabbage, very finely chopped
1 egg
25g chives, finely snipped
1–2cm piece fresh root ginger, finely grated, to taste
1 tablespoon soy sauce
1 tablespoon shaoxing rice wine (or dry sherry)
1 teaspoon salt
½ teaspoon white pepper, preferably freshly ground

for the dipping sauce
100ml soy sauce
2 tablespoons black vinegar or rice vinegar
2 teaspoons sesame oil
2 garlic cloves, crushed
a dash of chilli sauce, to taste (or use dried chilli flakes)

you will need
a large bamboo steamer (a regular steamer set over its own saucepan would be fine)

For the wrappers, weigh the flour into a bowl and gradually pour in 125ml cold water, stirring all the time, until you have a stiff dough, rough around the edges but with no loose flour. Turn on to the worktop and knead for 5 minutes until smooth. Wrap in cling film and chill in the fridge for at least 30 minutes.

In a large bowl, mix together the pork mince, cabbage, egg, chives, ginger, soy sauce, shaoxing wine, salt and white pepper. Leave to marinate for at least 30 minutes, or longer if possible; both the dough and the filling can be made and stored in the fridge for up to 24 hours.

Once the dough has rested, take it from the fridge and cut in half. Re-wrap one half and set aside. Take the other half of the dough and roll it into a long, thin sausage shape about 1cm in diameter. Cut in half, then cut in half again to give you 4 even-sized pieces. Take each piece and cut it into 5 even pieces, re-rolling each one briefly into a little ball as you go. Repeat with the other half of the dough to give you 40 balls in total.

Place a generous tablespoon of flour on a plate and have an empty plate ready alongside this. Take one ball, dip it in the flour and start to roll out into a circle, turning the dough through a quarter turn each time you roll to maintain its shape. You want to roll the dumpling wrappers as thin as you can, about 1–2mm, and approximately 9–10cm in diameter. Dip both sides of the wrapper briefly into the plate of flour again, then set aside on the second plate. Repeat with the rest of the dough balls, replenishing the flour as necessary.

Lay 10 wrappers out on the worktop in a couple of rows and have a little dish of cold water handy. Spoon a generous teaspoon of filling into the centre of each wrapper. Slide one into your hand and, using a clean finger, dab a little water around the edge of one half only. Begin to pleat and fold the unwatered side up and over the filling, pressing into the wet side as you go to stick it together. It will take a little practice and your first few might look a bit rough and ready, but they'll still taste great so stick with it! As long as the filling is completely enclosed it doesn't matter too much what it looks like.

Once it's all sealed, turn it crimp side pointing up, squeeze into a crescent shape and rest on a lightly floured baking sheet. Repeat with the other 9 wrappers, then lay out the next 10 wrappers, top with filling and repeat. Keep on going until you have used up all the filling and wrappers. You can freeze them at this point: space them out on a baking tray to freeze initially, then pack them into a bag or tub and leave in the freezer until ready to cook.

Make the dipping sauce by adding all the ingredients to a small bowl and stirring together.

When you are ready to cook, line the base of a large bamboo steamer with a circle of baking parchment, and tuck all the *jiaozi* inside, snugly but not touching each other. You may need to cook in 2 batches depending on the size of your steamer. Set over a wok of simmering water, making sure the water is lower than the bottom of the steamer, and cover with the lid. Steam for about 5–6 minutes, until the dumpling wrappers look translucent. If cooking from frozen, add 2–3 minutes to the cooking time.

Allow to cool for a couple of minutes before tucking in – but watch out as the filling gets mighty hot. Serve with the dipping sauce alongside.

China's answer to a sandwich, a *bao* is an exceedingly delicious steamed bun made from the softest, fluffiest white bread you have ever tasted. Here the buns are filled with succulent *char siu*, or barbecued pork. The recipe makes twice the amount of barbecued pork needed to fill the buns, but it's so tasty you'll have no trouble finding a use for it – either nibble it straight away or save it for stir fries. Or you could double the quantity of dough and make more *bao*. They freeze brilliantly, and you can cook them from frozen.

Note: you will need to begin this recipe at least 6 hours, or ideally 48 hours, before you want to eat, to allow the char siu to marinate.

CHAR SIU BAO

MAKES 12 BUNS

1.2kg skinless belly pork, cut into 4cm-thick strips
3 garlic cloves, crushed
3 tablespoons soy sauce
2 tablespoons oyster sauce
2 tablespoons tomato ketchup
2 tablespoons honey
2 tablespoons shaoxing rice wine (or dry sherry)
1 teaspoon Chinese five spice powder
1 teaspoon ground white pepper (ideally freshly ground)
3 spring onions, finely chopped
3cm piece fresh root ginger, grated
freshly ground black pepper

for the bao dough
500g strong white bread flour
250g cornflour
1 tablespoon caster sugar
1½ teaspoons baking powder
1 teaspoon fast-action yeast
1 teaspoon fine salt
450–500ml warm water

you will need
a large bamboo steamer (a regular steamer set over its own saucepan would be fine)

Hang a large zip-lock bag in a bowl to hold it open and put the belly pork strips inside. Add the garlic, soy sauce, oyster sauce, tomato ketchup, honey, rice wine, Chinese five spice powder and white pepper. Seal the bag and give everything a really good squish around to coat evenly in the marinade. Leave in the fridge to marinate for a minimum of 6 hours, or up to 48 hours if you have time.

Start the dough an hour or so before you want to assemble the buns. Tip the flours into a food mixer fitted with a dough hook and add the sugar, baking powder, yeast and salt. Mix together for a few seconds to combine. With the motor running slowly, start to pour in the water, adding just enough to bring it together as a soft ball. Knead for a few minutes until smooth and elastic. Alternatively, mix and knead by hand. Transfer to a clean, lightly oiled bowl, cover, and set aside at room temperature to prove for an hour.

Once the pork has marinated, fire up a barbecue to medium-hot. Use tongs to lift the ribs from the marinade and on to the grill. Cook for about 25 minutes, turning regularly until cooked through and lightly charred.

Meanwhile, pour the leftover marinade into a small saucepan and bring to the boil, cooking for a couple of minutes until thick and syrupy. Pour into a bowl and stir through the spring onions, ginger and a good grind of black pepper.

Once the pork has cooked, take half of it, about 2–3 slices, and chop into small (½–1cm) pieces, dropping these into the bowl of thickened marinade, onions and ginger as you go. Stir well to mix and set aside to cool a little while you roll the dough. Set the remaining pork aside for another meal – it will keep for up to 3 days in the fridge.

Tip the risen dough on to a lightly oiled worktop and roll into an 8–9cm-thick log. Cut into 12 even-sized slices and roll each into a ball. Use the palm of your hand to flatten each ball on the work surface to a disc about 5mm thick and 12–13cm in diameter.

Add a generous dessertspoon of filling to the centre of a disc of dough. Bring the sides up and over the top, pinching together like a little purse. Turn over so the *bao* is now seam-side-down, cupping gently to squeeze it into a neat ball shape. Repeat with the rest of the dough and filling, lining them up on a large plate or baking tray as you go.

Half fill a wok with water and set over a high heat to bring to a steady simmer. Take a bamboo steamer and line the base with baking parchment, pricking it all over with a small sharp knife so the steam can get through. Add 4 buns to the steamer, spacing out well, cover with the lid and carefully rest over the wok of simmering water. Steam for 15 minutes until the buns have puffed up. Slide the cooked buns on to a plate and steam the next 4 buns, then repeat with the last 4.

These buns are really hot when they first come out of the steamer, so leave them to cool for 10 minutes or so before eating, but they definitely taste best when warm so tuck in while you are steaming the last batch.

This warming Chinese soup is full of slippery homemade noodles surrounded by a full-flavoured anchovy stock. If you've never made noodles before, never fear, they are very easy. If you have a pasta machine you can use that for rolling and cutting the noodles; if not, just roll the dough as thin as you can and slice into strips with a small, sharp knife.

BANMIAN

SERVES 4

100g dried anchovies
3 garlic cloves, sliced
4 banana shallots, thinly sliced
   (reserve the peelings)
½ teaspoon white peppercorns
6 tablespoons vegetable oil
120g shiitake mushrooms, sliced
12 large raw king prawns,
   deveined
400g choi sum or pak choi,
   sliced into bite-sized pieces
a dash of sesame oil
4 eggs
salt and white pepper,
   preferably freshly ground, to
   taste
hot chilli sauce, to serve

for the noodles
250g plain flour, plus extra for
   dusting
2 tablespoons vegetable oil
1 egg
½ teaspoon fine salt

To make the noodles, add the flour, oil, egg, salt and 75ml cold water to a food mixer. Use the dough hook to mix together and knead until smooth, about 4–5 minutes. Alternatively, mix and knead by hand. Wrap tightly in cling film and rest in the fridge for an hour, or up to 24 hours.

In a large pan, add approximately two-thirds of the anchovies to 2 litres cold water. Add the garlic, the peelings from the shallots (they will give the soup a great colour) and the peppercorns. Set the pan over a medium heat and bring to the boil, then reduce the heat to a steady simmer and cook uncovered for an hour. Strain through a fine sieve into a clean pan, discarding the solids.

Place the vegetable oil in a wok and set over a high heat. Once hot, tip in the shallots and fry, stirring occasionally, until golden and crisp. Scoop out with a slotted spoon and drain on kitchen paper. Add the remaining anchovies and fry until crisp, again scooping out and draining on kitchen paper. Roughly chop and set aside.

To make the noodles, unwrap the chilled dough and cut into 4 even pieces, dusting each lightly in flour all over. If you have a pasta machine, roll each piece of dough as thinly as possible. Then switch to the cutting roller and cut into long, thin strips (like tagliatelle). Dust the noodles in more flour before mounding on to a plate or baking tray. Repeat with the other pieces of dough. If you are rolling by hand, dust the worktop and roll each piece into a long sheet, trying to get it as thin as possible. Then use a small, sharp knife to cut into strips, dusting them as you go and piling them on to the plate or baking tray.

Bring the strained stock back up to the boil and add the mushrooms. Simmer for a minute before adding the prawns and choi sum or pak choi. Simmer for another minute or two until the prawns are just turning pink all over. Add the noodles, stirring with a fork as you go to stop them from clumping, and let them simmer for a couple of minutes until almost tender but with a little bite. Season to taste with salt, white pepper and a little sesame oil.

Crack in the eggs, spacing them out as much as possible. Let them simmer, undisturbed, on top of the soup until they are just cooked to your liking – a minute or two for softly poached.

Serve the soup immediately in deep bowls, making sure everybody gets an egg, three prawns and plenty of noodles. Garnish with the fried shallots and crisp anchovy pieces, then some hot chilli sauce to shake over as you eat (or slurp!).

Egg toast is a ubiquitous Korean street breakfast, providing a nutritious and filling start to the day. The cheese and ham are lovely optional additions, but the brown sugar, unusual though it may seem, is pretty much essential to the egg toast experience.

EGG TOAST

SERVES 1; EASILY SCALED UP FOR A CROWD

2 eggs
½ carrot, grated
small handful of finely chopped white cabbage
25g unsalted butter
2 slices soft white bread
1 thin slice Cheddar cheese (optional)
1 thin slice ham (optional)
½ teaspoon soft brown sugar
tomato ketchup, to taste
chilli sauce, to taste
salt and freshly ground black pepper

Whisk the eggs in a small bowl, then add the carrot and cabbage and mix well. Season with a little salt and pepper. Set aside.

Melt half the butter in a small, preferably non-stick, frying pan. When it is foaming, add the slices of bread and, pressing down with a spatula, fry them until crisp. Turn over and fry on the other side until crisp. Remove to a plate and keep warm.

Add the rest of the butter to the pan and pour in the egg mixture, spreading it out evenly to an approximately toast-sized omelette. Cook over a medium-low heat for a few minutes until set, then use a fish slice to flip over. Lay the ham and cheese slices on top, if using, so that they warm a little, and cook for another minute until the egg is lightly crisp on the underside.

Lift the egg, ham and cheese on to one of the slices of toasted bread. Sprinkle over the brown sugar, followed by a good squirt of ketchup and chilli sauce, before topping with the other piece of toast. Cut in half if you like, or just grab it whole, and eat immediately.

Odeng is a type of fishcake from Korea that is most often served in a bowl of steaming broth – a particularly popular street food on chilly winter evenings. *Odeng* is commonly a flat sheet made from finely pulverised fish or seafood mixed with starch that is ribboned on to skewers. If you can't find them (try specialist Korean stores or online) then any shaped Chinese-style ready-made fishcake will be just fine

ODENG BROTH

SERVES 2 GENEROUSLY OR 4 AS PART OF A BIGGER MEAL

10 dried anchovies
½ onion, skin on (it gives a good colour to the broth)
200g daikon, peeled and cut into 4cm chunks
4 garlic cloves, peeled and bruised
1 teaspoon gochugaru (Korean red pepper powder)
10g fresh root ginger, cut into slices
2 tablespoons soy sauce
1 tablespoon rice wine vinegar
100g odeng (Korean fishcakes) (2 flat sheets)
4 spring onions, sliced on the diagonal, to serve
2 long red chillies, thinly sliced on the diagonal, to serve

you will need
4 bamboo skewers

Place the anchovies, onion, daikon, garlic, gochugaru and ginger in a large saucepan and pour in 1.5 litres cold water. Set over a medium-high heat and bring to the boil, then reduce the heat to a hearty simmer and cook, uncovered, for 30 minutes. Strain into a clean pan, discarding everything except the daikon. Add the daikon back into the broth, along with the soy sauce and rice wine vinegar.

Take one *odeng* sheet, cut it in half and weave lengthways on to a skewer. Repeat with the remaining fishcakes, and add all the skewers to the strained broth so the fishcakes are submerged. Simmer in the broth for 5 minutes until thoroughly heated through. Serve the broth in deep bowls, topped with the skewers and scattered with spring onion and red chilli.

Kimbap is the Korean equivalent of sushi and a street food staple. Pretty much anything goes for the filling so it's a great way of using up leftovers. Here I've kept it simple with mixed veg, but you could add strips of roast meat, flaked tuna or even crabsticks. Gochugaru is dried red pepper powder, with a hot, spicy and slightly smoky taste, and although *kimbap* would traditionally be served without a dipping sauce, this is a combination I just can't resist.

MIXED VEGETABLE KIMBAP WITH SPICY GOCHUGARU DIPPING SAUCE

MAKES ABOUT 40 KIMBAP, SERVING ABOUT 6

250g short grain white rice (sushi rice)
a pinch of salt
2 tablespoons rice wine vinegar
1 tablespoon toasted sesame oil, plus an extra 4 teaspoons
2 teaspoons toasted sesame seeds
2 eggs, lightly beaten with a little salt and pepper
100g carrots, cut into thin matchsticks
200g spinach, washed and shaken dry
5 sheets nori seaweed
125g pickled daikon, cut into thin matchsticks
freshly ground black pepper

for the gochugaru dressing
3 tablespoons dark soy sauce
1 tablespoon toasted sesame oil
1 teaspoon rice wine vinegar
3 teaspoons gochugaru (Korean red pepper powder)
1 teaspoon caster sugar
1 tablespoon toasted sesame seeds
1 garlic clove, crushed

you will need
a bamboo rolling mat

Tip the rice into a sieve and rinse well under cold running water, then add to a saucepan along with 375ml cold water and the salt. Set over a medium heat and bring to the boil, then cover with a lid and reduce the heat to a minimum, leaving to simmer for 15 minutes. Turn off the heat and rest, covered, for a further 15 minutes. Season the rice with the rice wine vinegar, 1 tablespoon sesame oil and toasted sesame seeds. Set aside while you prepare the fillings.

Make an omelette by adding 1 teaspoon sesame oil to a small frying pan and setting it over a high heat. When it's really hot, tip in the beaten egg, using a fork to scoop away the cooked edges from the sides of the pan to allow the uncooked egg to slide into contact with the base. If your pan is hot enough it should take less than a minute to cook. Slide on to a board and chop into 1cm strips. Set aside.

Wipe out the frying pan with kitchen paper, add another teaspoon of sesame oil and set back over the heat. Add the carrots and stir fry for a couple of minutes to soften a little. They should still have plenty of crunch. Set aside.

Add the damp spinach to a large saucepan and set over a medium heat. Cover with a tight-fitting lid and allow to wilt for a few minutes, stirring once or twice to make sure it wilts evenly. Allow to cool until you can handle it, then squeeze out as much water as possible. Chop roughly and drizzle over a teaspoon of sesame oil and season with a little grind of black pepper. Set aside.

Make the dressing by mixing all the ingredients together in a bowl.

When you are ready to roll, clear the worktop to give you plenty of space, and lay the bamboo mat in front of you, with the long side facing you. Lay a sheet of seaweed, shiny side down, on to the mat. Take a scoop of the seasoned rice and spread it in an even layer over the bottom two-thirds of the sheet, leaving a 1cm border all around. If you want to make sure you are dividing your pan of rice evenly, spread out all 5 sheets of seaweed and spread the rice out over all of them. You can then slide them on to the mat in turn.

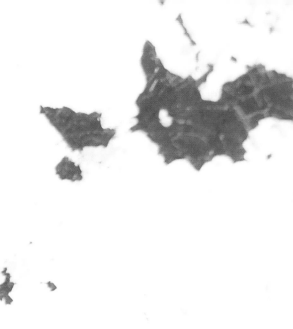

Now it's time to add the fillings – you want to line them up on the rice in neat rows, as close to each other as possible, starting with the carrots furthest away from you, leaving a 2cm margin of plain rice. Follow the carrots with the spinach, omelette and lastly the daikon.

To roll, begin at the edge nearest to you and roll up the mat over the rice, tucking the edge of the seaweed sheet over first. Keep rolling, using the mat to help you and pressing firmly as you go to squeeze everything together tightly into a sausage shape. Once you reach the other edge of the seaweed sheet, moisten it with a little dab of water before rolling all the way over to stick the seaweed together. It does take a little bit of practice, but once you get the hang of it you will work fast! Repeat with the remaining sheets and fillings.

Take a very sharp knife and use a piece of kitchen paper to dab a little sesame oil on to the blade. This will help prevent sticking. Slice each roll into generous 1cm pieces, re-oiling the knife every now and then.

Eat straight away with the dipping sauce alongside, or refrigerate until needed.

These tasty fried noodles – traditionally made using wheat and egg noodles rather than the soba (buckwheat noodles) that their name suggests – are ubiquitous all over Japan, where they are really popular for festivals, parties and just general speedy snacking. As with all stir fries, the time is in the chopping of ingredients; once everything is prepped and lined up in bowls; the cooking is done in a matter of minutes.

YAKISOBA NOODLES WITH PORK AND VEGETABLES

SERVES 2 GENEROUSLY

250g fresh ramen noodles or 125g thick dried egg noodles
1 tablespoon vegetable oil, plus 1 teaspoon
1 onion, thinly sliced
250g pork fillet, thinly sliced then cut into bite-sized pieces
150g green beans, topped, tailed and chopped into 3cm pieces
150g cabbage, shredded (I use Savoy; any is fine)
2 medium carrots, cut into thin batons
2 garlic cloves, sliced
aonori (powdered nori seaweed), to serve
benishoga strips (red pickled ginger), to serve

for the sauce
3 tablespoons soy sauce
2 tablespoons Worcestershire sauce
2 tablespoons mirin
1 tablespoon ketchup
1 tablespoon rice wine vinegar
1 teaspoon freshly ground black pepper

Cook the noodles according to the packet instructions. Drain well and toss a teaspoon of oil through to prevent them from clumping together. Set aside.

Mix together all the ingredients for the sauce in a small bowl and leave ready by the stove.

Add a tablespoon of oil to a large wok and set over a high heat. When it's smoking hot, add the onions and stir fry for 2 minutes. Add the pork fillet and stir fry for a further 3 minutes before tossing in the green beans, cabbage, carrots and garlic. Add 3 tablespoons of cold water and stir fry for another 4 minutes or so until the vegetables are tender but still with plenty of crunch. Pour in the sauce and stir fry for a minute before tossing in the cooked noodles and stirring until heated through.

Pile into bowls and serve immediately, sprinkled with the aonori and benishoga strips.

So popular are these chicken kebabs that in their home country of Japan they have whole take-out shops – or *yakitoriya* – dedicated to serving them. This version is flavoured with a classic soy-based *tare* sauce. It's traditional to cook these over a charcoal grill, and a barbecue is certainly the best way flavour-wise, but a ridged griddle pan on the hob will also give you pretty tasty results.

YAKITORI CHICKEN SKEWERS

MAKES 8 SKEWERS, SERVING 4

600g chicken thigh fillets, cut
  into 3cm cubes
6 spring onions, cut into 2cm
  lengths
1 tablespoon vegetable oil

for the tare sauce
100ml soy sauce
100ml mirin
100ml sake
1cm piece fresh root ginger,
  finely grated
2 teaspoons soft brown sugar

you will need
8 metal or bamboo skewers (if
  using bamboo, soak in cold
  water for an hour to prevent
  them from burning)

For the *tare* sauce, add all the ingredients to a small saucepan set over a medium-low heat and bring to the boil. Allow to simmer steadily until reduced by half in volume, about 15–20 minutes. Divide between 2 small dishes and set aside to cool. One dish is used as a dipping sauce, the other to glaze the skewers as they cook – dividing them prevents contamination from the raw meat as you are brushing with the glaze.

Thread the chicken and spring onions on to the skewers and brush all over with a little vegetable oil.

Fire up a barbecue until hot, or set a large ridged griddle pan over a high heat on the hob, then lay on the kebabs. Take one of the bowls of sauce and, using a brush, glaze the top of the kebabs. After a couple of minutes turn the kebabs over and brush with more sauce. Keep on turning and brushing the kebabs with sauce until cooked, around 10–12 minutes depending on the thickness of the chicken.

Serve the kebabs immediately with the second dish of sauce for dipping into.

Japan has turned taking food on the road into an art form. Every train station is filled with hundreds of options for eating on the go, from self-heating *bento* boxes to ready-to-drink soup in a can. This recipe combines two of my personal favourites – the famous Japanese *katsu-sando* (cutlet sandwich) and tender Japanese fried chicken.

TRIPLE-FRIED KARAAGE CHICKEN ROLLS WITH SEAWEED MAYONNAISE

Adam Liaw
MasterChef Australia, 2010 Champion

SERVES 6 AS A SNACK

400g chicken thigh fillets,
    skin-on, cut into 5cm pieces
60ml soy sauce
2 tablespoons sake
a pinch of caster sugar
1 teaspoon grated ginger
75g potato flour
vegetable oil, for deep frying
6 small soft rolls
200g very finely shredded white
    cabbage
a handful of watercress
1 small red onion, very finely
    chopped
1 teaspoon shichimi togarashi
    (Japanese seven spice pepper)
    (optional)
salt

for the seaweed mayonnaise
grated rind of 1 lemon, plus 1
    tablespoon lemon juice
1 tablespoon aonori (Japanese
    green dried seaweed)
250g Japanese mayonnaise

Place the chicken pieces in a bowl and add the soy sauce, sake and sugar. Squeeze the grated ginger between your fingers, adding the juice to the bowl and discarding the solids. Stir to coat and leave to marinate for about 5 minutes.

Place the potato flour in a large bowl and stir through a pinch of salt. Remove the chicken from the marinade with chopsticks and drop it into the flour, one piece at a time – adding the pieces one at a time stops you from pouring in too much of the marinade and prevents the chicken from sticking together. Coat the chicken in the flour, shake off any excess and set aside uncovered and out of the fridge while you heat the oil. This air-drying will create a crisper crust.

Half fill a large saucepan or wok with vegetable oil and heat to around 190°C/375°F. You may need to fry the chicken in 2 or 3 batches so that you don't reduce the temperature of the oil too much. Deep fry the chicken for a minute. Remove the chicken to a rack and leave to rest for 30 seconds. Return the chicken to the oil and fry for 30 seconds, and then rest on the rack for 30 seconds. Transfer the chicken back into the oil for one last blast of 30 seconds and then rest on the rack for 2 minutes, seasoning with ¼ teaspoon salt.

For the seaweed mayonnaise, mix all the ingredients together until well combined.

Cut the rolls in half and lightly toast them on the inside only. Fill with a little of the cabbage, watercress and onion. Add the fried chicken and mayonnaise and top with a little shichimi togarashi, if using.

Daigaku imo is a classic Japanese dish that literally means 'university potato', so-named because its inexpensive but wholesome and calorific ingredients have made it a perennial favourite among cash-strapped students. The flavour is sweet, but not overly so, which means it can be enjoyed both as a dessert or as an afternoon snack.

DAIGAKU IMO

 Tim Anderson
MasterChef UK, 2011 Champion

SERVES 2–4

1 large (or 2 small) sweet potatoes (ideally the purple-skinned, yellow-fleshed variety)
3 tablespoons vegetable oil
5 tablespoons caster sugar
¼ teaspoon soy sauce
grated zest of 1 lime, plus the juice of ½ lime
1 teaspoon black sesame seeds

Wash the sweet potato thoroughly (don't peel it) and cut it into irregular wedges no larger than 3cm thick. Soak the wedges in cold water for 20–30 minutes to remove the excess starch, then dry completely with kitchen paper or a clean tea towel.

Place the oil, sugar, soy sauce, lime zest and juice in a deep frying pan over a low heat and stir. Add the potatoes to the pan, toss to coat in the sugar mixture, and increase the heat to medium. Place a lid on the pan and leave to heat until you hear it sizzling. Turn the heat down to medium-low and cook for a further 2–3 minutes, then remove the lid and cook for another 10 minutes or so, turning the potatoes frequently to ensure they brown lightly on all sides. The potatoes are done when you can pierce them easily with a chopstick or butter knife.

When the potatoes are tender and nicely browned, turn off the heat and stir through the sesame seeds. Leave to cool slightly, then enjoy them on their own or with vanilla ice cream.

Native to Nepal, *momos* are little steamed dumplings, made in a very similar way to the Chinese *jiaozi* on page 222. The *momos* in this recipe are filled with delicately spiced minced chicken and served with an addictive pickled chilli chutney.

Note: you will need to begin this recipe the day before you want to eat, as the chillis need to soak overnight.

CHICKEN MOMOS WITH PICKLED CHILLI CHUTNEY

MAKES ABOUT 40 DUMPLINGS

350g chicken thigh fillets, roughly chopped
1 onion, roughly chopped
3 spring onions, roughly chopped
2 garlic cloves, chopped
1 tablespoon cumin seeds, toasted
¼ teaspoon ground nutmeg
a handful of fresh coriander
salt and freshly ground black pepper

for the wrappers
1 quantity jiaozi wrappers (see page 222)
flour, for dipping

for the pickled chilli chutney
12 dried red chillies, roughly chopped
2 tablespoons white wine vinegar
1 small onion, roughly chopped
2 medium ripe tomatoes, roughly chopped
3 garlic cloves

you will need
a large bamboo steamer (a regular steamer set over its own saucepan would be fine)

To make the chutney, add the chillies to a small bowl and pour over the vinegar. Leave to soak for at least 12 hours, ideally overnight.

Place the chillies and vinegar (which will have been mostly absorbed) in a food processor, along with the onion, tomatoes, garlic and a large pinch of salt. Process until smooth. Taste, adding a little more salt if needed and some black pepper. Scoop into a small bowl and set aside at room temperature.

To make the filling, place the chicken in a food processor and pulse until chopped. Add the onion, spring onion, garlic, cumin, nutmeg, coriander, ½ teaspoon salt and a little black pepper and pulse until you have a smooth paste. Scoop into a bowl, cover and chill for at least an hour for the flavours to develop; overnight is fine.

To make the dumpling wrappers, follow the *jiaozi* instructions on page 222, including rolling out, but the folding is different, so stop once you've rolled out 40 wrappers. Line up 10 wrappers in 2 rows on a lightly floured worktop. Have a little bowl of cold water handy, along with a plate of flour to dip the finished momos in.

Put a teaspoon of filling in the centre of each wrapper. Take one, placed either in the palm of one hand or in front of you on the worktop, and dab a little water around one half only. Begin to make tiny pleats around the filling, drawing the folds up to the top so they meet in the centre and stick together. Once you have pleated all the way round, give the pleats a little twist together in a clockwise direction to completely seal in the filling. Dip the base into the plate of flour and line up on a baking tray. Repeat with the remaining 9 wrappers, then lay out the next 10 wrappers and repeat. Do this until you have used up all 40 wrappers and filling. You can freeze them at this point: space them out on a baking tray to freeze initially, then pack them into a bag or tub and freeze until ready to cook.

When you are ready to cook, line the base of a large bamboo steamer with a circle of baking parchment, and tuck all the dumplings inside, snugly but not touching each other. You may need to cook in 2 batches depending on the size of your steamer. Set over a wok of simmering water, making sure the water is lower than the bottom of the steamer, and cover with the lid. Steam for about 5–6 minutes, until the dumpling wrappers look translucent. If cooking from frozen, add 2–3 minutes to the cooking time. Serve with the pickled chutney alongside.

An absolute classic Thai dish, cooked on roadsides throughout the land (and far, far beyond), this is a dish that cooks in moments, so get all the component parts lined up and ready before you fire up your wok.

PAD THAI

SERVES 2

150g dried flat rice noodles
1 heaped tablespoon dried shrimp
2 tablespoons tamarind water (made from 1 tablespoon tamarind concentrate mixed with 1 tablespoon warm water)
1 tablespoon soft brown sugar
2 tablespoons fish sauce
a pinch of dried chilli flakes, or more to taste
60g green beans, topped and tailed and cut into 2cm pieces
1 medium carrot, diced
1 tablespoon vegetable oil
2 spring onions, chopped
1 fat garlic clove, finely chopped
180g raw king prawns (shelled)
a handful of coriander, roughly chopped
2 eggs, lightly beaten with a little salt and pepper
100g beansprouts
60g peanuts, roughly chopped
lime wedges, to serve
sweet chilli sauce, to serve

Soak the noodles for an hour in cold water, drain and set aside. Place the dried shrimp in a small heatproof glass or mug and cover well with boiling water. Leave to soak for 15 minutes, then drain and roughly chop.

In a small bowl, mix together the tamarind water, sugar, fish sauce and chilli flakes. Stir well until the sugar has dissolved. Taste a tiny amount – it should be a good balance of sweet, sour and salty, with a little kick from the chilli. Adjust to taste with more of everything, going steady as it's easier to add than take away!

Blanch the green beans and carrots in boiling water for 3 minutes until tender but with plenty of bite. Drain and set aside.

Set a wok over a high heat and add the vegetable oil. When it's hot, add the spring onions, garlic, carrots, beans and raw prawns, stir frying for a couple of minutes until the prawns are just cooked.

Add the chopped dried shrimp and the tamarind water and stir fry for a further minute before tipping in the noodles and coriander, tossing until well coated. Push the noodles to one side of the wok and pour in the beaten egg, scrambling lightly until just set. Turn off the heat, add the beansprouts and half the peanuts and toss everything together.

Serve immediately in warmed bowls, scattered with the remaining peanuts. Serve with the lime wedges and sweet chilli sauce.

Lok lak is a fabulous hot beef salad from Cambodia that is usually served topped with a fried egg to make a really satisfying meal. I think of this as a fantastic after-work dish, as you can set the beef marinating in the morning, and then it takes just minutes to get to the eating stage when you are tired and hungry. The ravenous could add some steamed rice alongside. I use skirt steak as it's my favourite cut for succulence and flavour, but any will do.

Note: you will need to start this recipe several hours before you want to eat, or ideally the day before, to allow the beef to marinate.

BEEF LOK LAK

SERVES 2

350g beef skirt steak, sliced
    thinly across the grain (or use
    your favourite cut)
3 tablespoons soy sauce
1 tablespoon oyster sauce
1 tablespoon tomato ketchup
1 teaspoon fish sauce
2 garlic cloves, sliced
2 handfuls of soft lettuce leaves
2 ripe tomatoes, sliced
¼ cucumber, sliced
2 tablespoons vegetable oil
1 teaspoon cornflour, mixed to
    a paste with 1 teaspoon cold
    water
2 eggs
2 spring onions, thinly sliced
freshly ground black pepper

for the dressing
1 heaped teaspoon black
    peppercorns
juice of 1 lime
1 teaspoon fish sauce
1 teaspoon caster sugar

Place the beef strips in a non-metallic bowl and add the soy sauce, oyster sauce, tomato ketchup, fish sauce, garlic and a generous grind of black pepper. Stir thoroughly to mix, cover with cling film and leave in the fridge to marinate for a minimum of 2 hours, or ideally overnight.

Make the dipping sauce by grinding the peppercorns in a spice mill or pestle and mortar until finely ground. Mix in the lime juice, fish sauce and sugar, stirring well until the sugar has dissolved. Set aside.

Arrange the lettuce, tomato and cucumber over 2 plates.

Heat 1 tablespoon oil in a wok until smoking hot, then tip in the beef, stir frying for a few minutes until it is almost cooked to your liking. Quickly stir through the cornflour paste and thicken over a high heat for a further minute. Turn off the heat under the wok and keep warm.

Add the remaining oil to a frying pan and set over a medium-high heat. When it's hot, crack in the eggs and fry until cooked to your liking.

Arrange the beef on top of each plate of salad and top with a fried egg. Scatter over the spring onion, drizzle over the dressing and serve immediately.

Barbecuing is a big deal in Cambodia, with roadside 'Khmer BBQ' stalls and beer gardens all over the place, dishing up exquisitely grilled meat alongside pitchers of icy-cold beer. This recipe takes a load of juicy, meaty pork ribs and gives them the Cambodian flavour treatment with honey, ginger and lemongrass. Heaven. Just don't forget to chill the beer.

Note: you will need to start this recipe up to 24 hours before you want to eat, to allow the ribs time to marinate.

SLOW-GRILLED PORK RIBS WITH HONEY, GINGER AND LEMONGRASS

SERVES 4–6, DEPENDING ON GREED!

1.3kg meaty pork ribs
lime juice and wedges, to serve
2 or 3 red bird's-eye chillies, thinly sliced, to serve

for the marinade
80g fresh root ginger, roughly chopped
1 whole head of garlic, cloves peeled and roughly chopped
2 sticks lemongrass, outer leaves discarded, inner roughly chopped
4 tablespoons honey
4 tablespoons soy sauce
3 tablespoons fish sauce
1 tablespoon black peppercorns, coarsely ground

Hang a zip-lock bag in a bowl to hold it open and put the pork ribs inside. Add all the marinade ingredients to a deep jug and pulse with a stick blender until you have a smooth paste. Alternatively, whizz them all up in a food processor. Scoop the marinade into the bag and squidge the bag about to mix it through. Seal the bag tight and leave in the fridge for as long as possible, ideally overnight. If you can, turn the bag over a few times to keep the marinade circulating.

When you are ready to cook, fire up the barbecue. You want to cook the ribs slowly over a medium-low temperature, which is easy to control if you're using gas. With charcoal, the temperature is harder to control, so push the coals to one side of the barbecue and grill the ribs on the coal-free side. If you have a grill thermometer (one that rests directly on the grill bars), you want it to hover around 100°C (210°F).

Cook the ribs, turning regularly, until they are crisp and caramelised on the outside and tender within. Ideally this will take about an hour or so if the heat is nice and low. To serve, pile the ribs into a dish, squeeze over some lime juice and scatter with the chopped chillies.

Pepper is commonly used in Cambodian cooking for adding pungent heat, as their cuisine predates the arrival of chillies into Asia. It's worth seeking out fresh green peppercorns for this speedy stir fry, as they add an exquisite, almost floral fragrance and a subtle heat that is a bit lost with the pickled ones in jars; they are reasonably easy to find in Thai or Asian grocery shops or online. This recipe uses them in abundance, just as they would in Cambodia, but do halve the quantity for a milder dish.

PORK AND GREEN PEPPERCORNS

SERVES 2

350g pork fillet
50g green peppercorns
2 tablespoons vegetable oil
6 spring onions, sliced on the diagonal
3 garlic cloves, thinly sliced
3 tablespoons dark soy sauce
2 teaspoons fish sauce
2 teaspoons oyster sauce
1 teaspoon soft brown sugar
steamed rice, to serve

Slice the pork fillet down the length to give you 2 long pieces. Wrap each in cling film and place in the freezer for 30–45 minutes to harden up – this helps you to cut it very thinly. Remove from the freezer, unwrap and slice very thinly across the grain in 2mm strips.

Bruise the green peppercorns, either with the flat of a large knife or by crushing gently in a pestle and mortar, so they crack open a little and release their aroma.

Add the oil to a wok and set over a high heat. Once hot, add the pork and peppercorns and stir fry for a couple of minutes, allowing the meat to colour a little in places. Add the spring onions and garlic and fry for a further couple of minutes. Finally add the soy sauce, fish sauce, oyster sauce and sugar, along with a couple of tablespoons of water, and stir fry for a minute or two until the sauce is rich and thick.

Serve immediately with plenty of steamed rice.

Packed full of vibrant herbs and leaves, these fresh uncooked spring rolls are sometimes known as 'summer rolls' and it's easy to see why. This version uses prawns for simplicity, but traditionally, in Vietnam, they would have a combination of pork and prawns. Feel free to experiment with the protein part of the filling: you could use a little leftover chicken or roast pork or even add a scattering of chopped roasted peanuts, but don't scrimp on the herbs and lettuce, they are essential to the 'summery-ness'.

GOI CUON WITH NUAC CHAM

MAKES 12 SPRING ROLLS, SERVING 4–6

1 teaspoon salt
18 large raw prawns
120g dried rice vermicelli
1 soft lettuce, leaves separated and cut in half, hard central ridge removed
1 medium carrot, grated
a handful of mint leaves
a handful of coriander leaves
12 long chives, snipped in half
12 large (22cm) rice spring roll wrappers

for the nuoc cham dipping sauce
juice of 2 limes
2 tablespoons fish sauce
2 garlic cloves, finely chopped
2–3 teaspoons caster sugar, to taste
1 or 2 red bird's-eye chillies, finely chopped (remove seeds for a milder sauce)
1cm piece fresh root ginger, finely grated to a paste

Make the dipping sauce by mixing all the ingredients together in a small bowl. Start with a lesser quantity of sugar, adding a little more to taste. It should be a good balance of sour, sweet, salty and sharp. Set aside for the flavours to mingle.

Bring a small saucepan of water to the boil, adding the salt as it heats up. When it's boiling, drop in the prawns, reduce the heat to a gentle simmer and poach for just long enough for them to turn completely pink, about 1–2 minutes. Drain and allow them to cool a little. Slice in half lengthways and set aside.

Add the rice vermicelli to a bowl and pour over enough boiling water to cover well. As it begins to soften, stir with a fork to separate the noodles. Leave for 4 minutes until soft but with a little bite. Drain well and rinse under cold running water to stop further cooking. Set aside.

To make the spring rolls, line up the fillings – cooked prawns, lettuce, vermicelli, carrot and herbs – in small bowls on a clean work surface.

Fill a deep plate or shallow bowl (big enough to fit a single rice wrapper in a flat, crease-free layer) with cold water next to the fillings. Take a rice wrapper and lay it in the water, submerging it completely for 1–2 minutes, just long enough for it to be pliable but not too soft. Remove immediately and lay flat in front of you on the worktop. Take 3 halves of prawns and lay them cut side up in a line down the centre. Take a couple of halves of lettuce leaves and roll up into a cigar shape, placing on top of the prawns. Add a little clump of rice vermicelli on top of this, again in a cigar shape, and sprinkle on a big pinch of grated carrot. Top with a generous scatter of mint and coriander, and lay on 2 pieces of chive. Bring the bottom edge of the wrapper tightly up over the filling, then fold up the sides so that the filling is snugly contained at each end. Roll up tightly, squeezing out the air as you go, so that everything is completely sealed. Transfer to a plate. Repeat with the remaining wrappers and fillings.

To serve, slice each roll in half on the diagonal and serve with the dipping sauce alongside.

Banh xeo roughly translates as 'sizzling cakes', named after the noise of the batter hitting the oil in the hot pan. And that pan needs to be *really* hot for best effect. These thin and crispy pancakes are a glorious yellow thanks to the turmeric, and filled with a rich mix of garlicky mushrooms and roast chicken. Plenty of herbs and a traditional dipping sauce give a fresh authentic Vietnamese flavour.

BANH XEO WITH CHICKEN AND MUSHROOM

MAKES 4 PANCAKES

2 tablespoons vegetable oil
1 onion, thinly sliced
250g shiitake mushrooms, sliced
2 garlic cloves, crushed
2 handfuls of leftover roast chicken
a handful of beansprouts
a handful of mint leaves
a handful of coriander leaves
2 spring onions, sliced into thin matchsticks
salt and freshly ground black pepper
1 quantity of nuoc cham dipping sauce (see page 257), to serve

for the pancakes
125g rice flour
1 heaped teaspoon ground turmeric
1 teaspoon salt
1 x 400ml can coconut milk

Make the pancake batter by weighing the flour into a large bowl and stirring through the turmeric and salt. Pour in the coconut milk and start to add some cold water, about 200ml or so, whisking continuously until you have a smooth batter. It should be the consistency of double cream. Cover with cling film and set aside at room temperature for a couple of hours to rest.

When you are ready to cook, add a tablespoon of oil to a frying pan and set over a medium heat. Add the onion and stir fry for 3 minutes, then add the mushrooms and a seasoning of salt and pepper and stir fry for a few minutes until they are starting to soften. Add the garlic and cook for another minute, then tip in the shredded chicken and stir fry for a further minute until hot. Keep warm while you make the pancakes.

In another frying pan (preferably non-stick) add a drizzle of oil and set over a high heat. You need to leave the pan to get really hot. When you think it's hot enough, give it another 30 seconds or so to be sure. Give the batter a quick mix through – it will have thickened up a bit, so whisk through a little more cold water to take it back to double cream consistency. Then pour a ladleful into the pan, swirling it about so it spreads out to form a thin pancake. Cover the pan with a lid or snuggly fitting foil and leave to cook for about 3 minutes. The underside of the pancake should be really crisp and the edges coming away from the pan. Use a fish slice to transfer to a serving plate then spoon a quarter of the mushroom and chicken filling on to one half. Scatter over some beansprouts, herbs and spring onions before folding over to cover.

Repeat with the remaining batter and filling to make 3 more pancakes. Eat while still hot, with the nuoc cham dipping sauce served alongside.

This spicy lemongrass beef soup was my favourite Vietnamese noodle soup growing up, a dish my mother would make on occasional Sundays. I wasn't keen on eating it spicy as a child, so my mother fed me the milder version, but now I love the extra heat. It's a perfect balance of sweet, sour, spicy and savoury. In Vietnam, you can find this dish anywhere from noodle shops to street stalls to a home kitchen.

BUN BO HUE

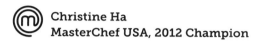
Christine Ha
MasterChef USA, 2012 Champion

SERVES 8

900g beef bones
900g pork bones
900g beef shin
1 beef shin tendon (optional)
450g pork hock
1 onion, thinly sliced
4 tablespoons fish sauce
2 tablespoons vegetable oil
1 teaspoon cayenne pepper
1 teaspoon shrimp paste, diluted
  in cold water
2 stalks lemongrass, white
  parts bruised and sliced
  lengthways; green parts made
  into a bouquet garni
1 teaspoon granulated sugar
675g medium thick rice
  vermicelli
salt and freshly ground black
  pepper
6 spring onions, thinly sliced, to
  garnish
small bunch of coriander, finely
  chopped, to garnish

to serve
purple cabbage, thinly sliced
lime wedges
shrimp paste

First, prepare the bones and meats. Sprinkle generously with salt, leave for a maximum of 15 minutes, then rinse with cold water and use the salt granules to scrub away any impurities.

Bring a stockpot of lightly salted water to the boil and parboil the bones and meats for 2 minutes, then drain. Trim the meats, reserving the beef tendon, if using, for the soup. Cut the beef into slices approximately 6cm long and 5mm thick. In a large bowl, mix together the sliced beef, half the onion and 1 tablespoon fish sauce, and season with pepper.

In a clean stockpot over a medium-high heat, heat the oil and sauté the remaining onion until fragrant. Add the cayenne and beef mixture, stirring frequently. Stir in the shrimp paste, lemongrass and reserved beef tendon, lower the heat to medium and sauté until the beef is browned all over. Return the bones and pork to the pot, cover with water (around 7 litres) and bring to the boil. Add the remaining fish sauce, sugar, and salt to taste. Reduce the heat and simmer for approximately 3 hours, partially covered, until the beef and pork are tender. Remove the meats and simmer the bones for another hour. Remove and discard the bones.

Towards the end of the simmering time, cook the noodles according to the packet instructions, until al dente.

Ladle the soup over the noodles, beef and pork. Garnish with the spring onion and coriander, and serve with the cabbage, lime wedges and shrimp paste.

Like most kebabs, these squid skewers taste best when cooked over a really hot barbecue, so do cook them outside if you can. The sauce makes a lovely change from the ubiquitous peanut-based sauces and is based on *kecap manis*, a deliciously addictive sweet soy sauce from Indonesia and Malaysia.

SATE SOTONG WITH SAMBAL KECAP

MAKES 4 LARGE OR 8 SMALLER KEBABS

500g squid (a big one, or several smaller ones), cleaned
1 teaspoon cumin seeds
1 teaspoon coriander seeds
25g fresh root ginger, finely grated
juice of 1 lime
1 garlic clove, crushed
1 teaspoon soft brown sugar
1 tablespoon vegetable oil
1 tablespoon soy sauce
salt and freshly ground black pepper, to taste
lime wedges, to serve

for the sambal kecap
5 tablespoons kecap manis (sweet soy sauce)
1 tablespoon light soy sauce
4 bird's-eye chillies, finely chopped
2 garlic cloves, crushed
1 shallot, very finely chopped
zest and juice of 1 lime

you will need
4–8 metal or bamboo skewers (if using bamboo, soak in cold water for an hour to prevent them from burning)

Remove and discard the outer membrane from the squid, or ask your fishmonger to do it for you, if you prefer. Give the squid a really good rinse in cold running water, inside and out, as there is often some grit lurking deep in the body cavity. Slice off the two wings and cut into 2cm strips, then slice the body into 2cm rings and place all the pieces in a large bowl.

Place the cumin and coriander in a small frying pan and toast over a medium heat for a minute or two until you can smell their aroma wafting up from the pan. Tip into a spice mill or pestle and mortar and grind to a powder. Mix the ground spices with the rest of the ingredients, except the lime wedges, and pour over the squid, stirring thoroughly until well coated. Set aside to marinate at room temperature for 20–30 minutes.

For the *sambal kecap*, combine all the ingredients in a small bowl.

When you are ready to cook, fire up the barbecue to get it really hot. You can also cook over a really hot griddle pan. Thread the squid on to skewers and cook for 2 minutes each side until slightly charred. Eat immediately with the sauce drizzled over or alongside for dipping, and the lime wedges for squeezing.

With its unusual combination of tropical fruit and sour-sweet dressing of tamarind and shrimp paste, *rojak* can be something of an acquired taste. The first bite will take you by surprise, but it soon becomes slightly addictive, hitting all the salty, sweet, sour, savoury and umami senses. This is one of the top street food snacks of Malaysia, where it's often served in cones made of newspaper lined with a banana leaf.

ROJAK SALAD

SERVES 6–8

1 Granny Smith apple
½ pineapple, cut into bite-sized pieces
1 firm mango, cut into bite-sized pieces
1 Asian pear, cut into bite-sized pieces
½ cucumber, cut into bite-sized pieces
3 or 4 large banana leaves, shaped into cones (optional)
75g roasted salted peanuts, chopped
2 or 3 bird's-eye chillies, finely sliced (optional)

for the dressing
15g shrimp paste
50g jaggery, roughly chopped
3 tablespoons kecap manis (sweet soy sauce)
85g tamarind pulp, mixed to a paste in 100ml boiling water
1 teaspoon chilli powder

you will need
bamboo skewers

For the dressing, spread the shrimp paste in a thin layer on a small sheet of kitchen foil and wrap up to make a little package. Set a small frying pan over a high heat and, once hot, add the foil pack and toast for a minute on each side. Lift out and allow to cool. Turn off the heat – the pan will be very hot – and add the jaggery and *kecap manis*, stirring quickly as the jaggery melts in the residual heat. Strain the tamarind paste through a sieve into the pan and add the chilli powder. Unwrap the toasted shrimp paste and scrape it into the pan. Set the pan back over a medium heat and cook for a couple of minutes, stirring constantly, until thick and glossy. Pour into a bowl and set aside to cool.

Chop the apple into bite-sized pieces and combine with the other prepared fruits and cucumber in a large serving bowl or banana leaf cones, if using. Drizzle over the dressing and scatter with the chopped peanuts and chillies, if using. Serve immediately, using bamboo skewers to pick up the pieces of fruit.

This fried radish cake with prawns, beansprouts and duck eggs is one of my favourite street foods in Malaysia. I usually track one down in the weekly night markets known as Pasar Malam. If you visit a night market anywhere in Malaysia, remember to wear loose-fitting clothes, bring an empty stomach and a sense of adventure. Try everything. What makes this dish such a joy to eat is the combination of crisp exterior and soft interior with crunchy vegetables and juicy prawns popping in your mouth. Radish cake is also great fried in slices until crisp and topped with poached or fried eggs and bacon for an alternative breakfast.

CHAI TAU KUEH

 Ping Coombes
MasterChef UK, 2014 Champion

SERVES 4

1 tablespoon vegetable oil
2 garlic cloves, diced
2 garlic chives or spring onions, cut into strips
180g raw king prawns
2 tablespoons preserved turnip (optional)
2 duck eggs, beaten
180g beansprouts

for the radish cake
600g radish/daikon or turnip, grated
4 tablespoons vegetable oil
1 Chinese sausage or 8 rashers smoked streaky bacon, finely diced
2 spring onions, chopped
230g rice flour
1 tablespoon cornflour
½ teaspoon caster sugar
½ teaspoon salt

for the seasoning
2 teaspoons dark soy sauce
1 teaspoon light soy sauce
2 teaspoons kecap manis (sweet soy sauce)
1½ tablespoons fish sauce
¼ teaspoon caster sugar
large pinch of ground white pepper
1 tablespoon Sriracha sauce (optional)

For the radish cake, place the grated radish or turnip in a wok or saucepan with 250ml water and bring to the boil. Lower the heat and simmer for 10 minutes until the water has slightly evaporated and the radish has a slushy consistency. Remove from the wok and set aside in a separate bowl.

Clean the wok, then heat 2 tablespoons vegetable oil and fry the bacon or Chinese sausage with the spring onions for about 5 minutes. Tip the cooked radish into the wok, mix well and add the rice flour, cornflour, sugar and salt. Working quickly, mix well and keep the mixture moving around the wok to cook the flour for about 5 minutes. Turn off the heat.

Choose a dish big enough to fit into the wok and oil it with a little vegetable oil. Tip the radish mixture into the dish and pack it down with the back of a spoon. Smooth the top as much as possible. Place the dish on top of a steam rack over the wok, fill the wok below with water, bring to the boil, cover and steam on a high heat for 45 minutes. Check the level of water often so that it doesn't run dry. Remove the cake from the heat and leave to cool. Place in the fridge for about 2 hours or overnight. This will ensure the cake is firm enough to cut.

Take 450g of the radish cake and cut it into 2.5cm strips and then into 1.25cm cubes. The remaining cake can be frozen for 2 months, or kept in the fridge for another 2 days and fried up for breakfast (see introduction)!

Heat the remaining vegetable oil in a wok or saucepan over a medium heat and fry the cake cubes until brown and crisp, about 10 minutes. Place them in a separate bowl.

Mix all the seasoning ingredients together in a small bowl.

Using the same wok or saucepan, heat the vegetable oil and add the garlic and chives or spring onions and fry for a minute. Add the prawns and preserved turnip, if using, and fry until the prawns start to turn pink. Add the cubes of radish cake along with the seasoning mix, and make sure they are well incorporated. Pour the eggs over the mixture like an omelette and let it sit for a minute. Add the beansprouts and stir fry the mixture for about 2 minutes, until the eggs are cooked through. Serve immediately with more Sriracha, if desired.

Chilli lime syrup adds a great kick to these comforting Malaysian banana fritters. Although it's not traditional, I just love to add a dollop of vanilla ice cream to the top of each hot fritter before I drizzle over the sauce. Best eaten with your fingers, but be quick – the combination of melting ice cream and sauce makes this a messy business!

PISANG GORENG WITH CHILLI SYRUP

SERVES 6 GENEROUSLY

100g rice flour
100g cornflour
2 teaspoons baking powder
175ml ice-cold water
6 bananas
vanilla ice cream, to serve
   (optional)

for the chilli syrup
150g caster sugar
grated zest and juice of 2 limes
1 to 3 bird's-eye chillies, finely
   sliced, to taste

For the chilli syrup, place the sugar, lime zest and juice and chillies in a small pan and set over a medium heat. Bring to the boil and simmer for 3 minutes, then remove from the heat and pour into a small bowl. Set aside to cool. The chillies will float to the surface as it cools; simply mix back through just before serving.

To make the batter for the fritters, stir together the rice flour, cornflour and baking powder in a bowl. Gradually pour in the ice-cold water, whisking as you go, until you have a smooth batter.

To prepare the bananas, peel and slice them in half lengthways, then chop each half in 2 so you get 4 wedges from each banana. Drop into the batter and stir to coat.

Preheat the oil in a deep fat fryer to 180°C/350°F. Give the bananas a last stir to make sure they are well coated, then drop into the oil, about 4–6 pieces at a time. Fry for about 4–5 minutes until crisp and golden, then drain on kitchen paper while you fry the remaining batches of banana.

Serve immediately with a dollop of ice cream, if using, and a drizzle of chilli syrup.

Along with curry laksa, this is one of Singapore's greatest street foods. The chicken is poached with utter simplicity, and the flavour of the dish is all about the chicken, so this is the time to use the best slow-reared bird you can afford. A chicken of a good age will have naturally matured bones, and these add to the flavour of the stock, which in turn adds oomph to the rice that is cooked in it.

HAINANESE CHICKEN RICE

SERVES 6–8

2kg chicken, preferably free range and organic
1 tablespoon sea salt flakes
100g fresh root ginger, thinly sliced, plus 30g finely grated
a bunch of spring onions, each cut into 3 pieces
1 tablespoon whole white peppercorns
500g jasmine rice
1 tablespoon vegetable oil
1 tablespoon sesame oil
2 banana shallots, finely chopped
4 garlic cloves, crushed
a small bunch of coriander, chopped, to serve
½ cucumber, thinly sliced, to serve
dark soy sauce, to taste
sesame oil, to taste

for the chilli sauce

100g medium-hot red chillies, roughly chopped (remove the seeds for less heat)
30g fresh root ginger, roughly chopped
1 banana shallot, roughly chopped
2 garlic cloves, chopped
juice of 1 lime
4 tablespoons chicken stock
2 teaspoons caster sugar, or to taste
salt, to taste

Set the chicken on a plate and rub all over with the sea salt, massaging it well into the skin. Stuff the sliced ginger and spring onions into the cavity, pushing them down well. Some may come out when the chicken is simmering, which is fine as it adds flavour to the stock. Set the chicken breast side down in a stockpot and add the peppercorns. Add just enough cold water to cover the chicken and set over a high heat to bring to the boil, skimming off any scum that rises to the surface. As soon as it starts boiling, reduce the heat to a minimum – you want to see the barest of bubbles popping at the surface – and simmer very gently until the chicken is cooked through. This will take about 30 minutes. A meat thermometer is handy here: insert it into the thickest part of the thigh – the chicken is cooked when it reads 75°C/170°F. Using two large spoons, carefully lift the chicken on to a plate. According to your preference, allow it to cool, or wrap it in foil and keep warm. At this point you can turn up the heat and reduce the cooking liquor to a more concentrated stock for use later – it will take a good 30 minutes on a hard boil to reduce it by half.

Meanwhile, place the rice in a bowl and cover well with cold water. Leave to soak while the chicken is poaching. Take a medium saucepan and add the vegetable oil and sesame oil and set over a medium-low heat. Add the shallots and fry gently for 10 minutes until starting to soften and colour. Stir through the grated ginger and garlic and fry for another couple of minutes before turning off the heat and setting aside until the chicken has finished cooking.

Once the chicken is cooked, drain the rice and add to the pan with the shallot mixture. Set over a medium-high heat and stir for 30 seconds or so to coat each grain in the oil, then ladle over just enough hot stock to cover the rice by a couple of millimetres. Bring to the boil, cover with a lid and boil for 5 minutes. Turn off the heat, leave the lid untouched and allow to steam undisturbed for 10 more minutes. Remove the lid and fork through the grains to separate a little.

To make the chilli sauce, place all the ingredients in a mini food processor and whizz to a sauce. You can also place all the ingredients in a deep jug and pulse with a stick blender. Spoon into a dish and set aside.

When you are ready to serve, chop the chicken into pieces using a large, heavy knife – it is normally served on the bone, but carve it like a roast chicken if you prefer. Serve the chicken on a bed of rice, scattered with a little chopped coriander, with the cucumber, chilli sauce, soy sauce and sesame oil alongside.

I adore this coconut-rich laksa soup, which has just the right balance between creamy comfort and heady spice. Curry laksa is perhaps *the* iconic street food of Singapore and is considered something of a national dish, although with its Malay/Chinese roots its popularity is widespread throughout South-East Asia.

PRAWN CURRY LAKSA

SERVES 4

750ml light chicken stock
400ml coconut milk
1 tablespoon soft brown sugar
400g raw king prawns
250g ready-cooked rice noodles
  (ideally thick ones)
salt

for the laksa spice paste
1 teaspoon dried shrimp
1 tablespoon coriander seeds
3 shallots, roughly chopped
3 garlic cloves, roughly chopped
1 teaspoon shrimp paste
2 stalks lemongrass, finely
  chopped
20g fresh root ginger, roughly
  chopped
20g galangal, roughly chopped
30g fresh turmeric root, roughly
  chopped
25g candlenuts or macadamia
  nuts
2–3 teaspoons dried chilli
  flakes, to taste
4 tablespoons vegetable oil

to garnish
3 hard-boiled eggs, peeled and
  cut into quarters or sliced
6 spring onions, thinly sliced
½ cucumber, sliced into thin
  matchsticks
3 red bird's-eye chillies, thinly
  sliced
a handful of fresh mint leaves,
  chopped
a handful of fresh coriander
  leaves, chopped
1 lime, cut into wedges
  (optional)

For the spice paste, first soak the shrimp in cold water for 15 minutes, then drain.

Next place the coriander seeds in a small frying pan and set over a medium heat to toast for a minute or so until you can smell their aroma wafting up from the pan. Tip into a spice mill or pestle and mortar and grind to a powder. Add to a mini food processor along with the remaining spice paste ingredients and whizz to a smooth paste.

When you are ready to make the soup, add the spice paste to a large saucepan and fry gently over a medium-low heat for a couple of minutes, or until fragrant. Add the stock, coconut milk and sugar, bring to the boil, reduce the heat to a simmer and cook for 10 minutes.

While the base is simmering, butterfly the prawns by running a sharp knife down the back of each to create an incision about 3mm deep from the top to the tail. Once the soup has had its initial simmer, drop the prawns in and cook gently for 3–4 minutes until they are just cooked and pink all the way through. Carefully stir in the cooked noodles and allow them to warm through. Add a little salt to taste.

Serve in deep bowls, with the garnishes arranged over each bowl.

Oyster omelette is one of my favourite comfort dishes – crisp and fluffy egg, chewy and crunchy potato starch, plump oysters and the spice of the *sambal* that is unique to each and every street food vendor. It is, in my opinion, one of the harder dishes to get right in the street food repertoire, much like the understated elegance and difficulty of the French omelette or the Japanese *dashimaki tamago*. My version actually borrows from both Thai and Singaporean methods of frying omelettes. Pouring the egg mixture from a height to deep fry in a pan or wok means that it puffs up and gets incredibly crisp in multiple spots in the pan, while the addition of potato starch mixes chewiness into the crispy deep-fried egg.

OYSTER OMELETTE

 Woo Wai Leong
MasterChef Asia, 2015 Champion

SERVES 2

vegetable oil, for frying
3 eggs
2 tablespoons fish sauce
10g rice starch
10g potato starch
6–8 medium-sized oysters (or more/fewer, to your preference), drained and juices reserved (you need 60ml oyster juices – top up with water if insufficient)
3 tablespoons olive oil
a handful of coriander
a handful of watercress or rocket (for a peppery bite)
sea salt

for the sambal
40g garlic, minced
1 teaspoon salt
100g long red chillis
1–2 teaspoons white vinegar
juice of 3 limes
15g caster sugar
20g vegetable oil, plus extra for brushing

For the *sambal*, place the garlic and salt in a pestle and mortar and combine into a paste. Brush the red chillis with oil and sear in a frying pan over a high heat until both sides are on the blacker side of brown, then set aside to cool. If you wish, cut the chillis in half lengthways and remove as many seeds as suits your tolerance (I remove about half).

In a blender or pestle and mortar, place the garlic paste and chillis, along with the remaining *sambal* ingredients, and grind to a smooth paste, adding a little water if needed. Taste, and balance the seasoning with salt, sugar or lime juice. Set aside.

Heat at least 5cm of oil in a semi-deep cast-iron pan or wok (a heavy-bottomed saucepan is also ideal) to around 180°C/350°F. Whisk the eggs and the fish sauce in a bowl until aerated and light blond in colour. In a separate bowl, whisk the two starches and the oyster juices.

This is the difficult/fun bit: whisking one more time, pour the egg mixture into the hot oil from a height of about 20cm above the level of the oil. The egg mixture will puff up and begin frying. Scrape the circumference of the pan with a wooden spoon/heatproof spatula to prevent it from sticking. After about 2 minutes, or when the bottom of the omelette starts to set and take on colour, give the starch mixture a final whisk and pour it randomly into the egg mixture. The mixture will sink through the top layer and settle on the bottom here and there. Continue frying until the base of the omelette starts to brown.

Flip the omelette carefully to cook the other side; cut the omelette, if necessary, to ease flipping. Once the other side starts to brown, remove the omelette from the pan and leave to rest on kitchen paper for about 5 minutes in a warm oven (about 110°C/90°C/Gas Mark ¼), to wick away as much oil as possible.

Remove any bits still left in the cast-iron pan or wok and drain the oil. Add the oysters to the pan and place over a medium heat. The oysters should firm up in the heat but still have a raw bite to them; it should not take more than 2 minutes. When the oysters have firmed up and are still juicy and plump, add 1–2 tablespoons *sambal* and toss to combine, then set the oysters aside to rest.

In a bowl, whisk 1 tablespoon of *sambal* with the olive oil until well incorporated, to make a vinaigrette. Dress the coriander and watercress or rocket with the vinaigrette and toss to combine.

Scatter the oysters and dressed salad over the omelette, as you would a pizza, and sprinkle with sea salt flakes to reinforce the seasoning. Serve!

Ayam is Indonesian for 'chicken', and this classic *sate* is best cooked over coals on a barbecue for maximum flavour. I think the very best thing about *sate ayam* is the delicious spiced peanut sauce served alongside, so this recipe makes a generous bowlful.

Note: this dish ideally needs to be started the day before so the chicken has plenty of time to marinate.

SATE AYAM WITH PEANUT SAUCE

MAKES 8 LARGE OR 16 SNACK-SIZED KEBABS, SERVING 4 AS A MAIN COURSE OR MORE AS A SNACK

1 tablespoon coriander seeds
600g chicken thigh fillets, cut into 2cm cubes
½ teaspoon ground turmeric
2 garlic cloves, crushed
1 banana shallot, very finely chopped
2 tablespoons kecap manis (sweet soy sauce)
1 tablespoon dark soy sauce
a generous grind of black pepper
¼ cucumber, cut into thin matchsticks, to serve
1–2 hot red chillies, chopped, to serve

for the peanut sauce
1 tablespoon vegetable oil
2 banana shallots, finely chopped
2 garlic cloves, crushed
1cm piece fresh root ginger, minced
1 stalk lemongrass, outer leaves discarded, inner finely minced (a spice mill is ideal for this)
½ teaspoon shrimp paste
125g roasted salted peanuts

100g creamed coconut, grated and dissolved in 250ml boiling water; or 250ml ready-made coconut milk
1 tablespoon soy sauce
1–2 teaspoons soft brown sugar
juice of ½ lime

you will need
8–16 metal or bamboo skewers (if using bamboo, soak in cold water for an hour to prevent them from burning)

Place the coriander seeds in a small frying pan and dry fry for 30 seconds or so until you can smell their aroma wafting up from the pan, then tip into a spice mill or pestle and mortar and grind to a coarse powder. Add to a bowl along with the diced chicken, turmeric, garlic, shallot, *kecap manis*, soy sauce and black pepper. Stir well until mixed, cover and set aside to marinate in the fridge for a couple of hours, or overnight if you prefer.

To make the peanut sauce, place the vegetable oil in a small saucepan and set over a medium heat. Add the shallot, garlic, ginger and lemongrass, frying for around 10 minutes until the shallot is translucent, reducing the heat if it's catching a little. Add the shrimp paste and stir to combine.

Coarsely grind the peanuts in a food processor or pestle and mortar. Tip into the saucepan, along with the coconut milk, soy sauce and 1 teaspoon sugar. Bring to the boil and simmer steadily, stirring often, for 5 minutes until the sauce has thickened. Season to taste with a squeeze of lime juice and a little more sugar. Keep warm over a low heat.

When you are ready to cook, fire up the barbecue. Thread the chicken on to skewers and grill or barbecue over hot coals for around 6–8 minutes until cooked through. Serve with the peanut sauce, cucumber and chopped chilli.

Pepes is a traditional Indonesian method of cooking food wrapped snugly in a banana leaf, and *ikan* means 'fish'. Here, then, is a delicious recipe for delicately spiced fish fillets barbecued inside pieces of banana leaf. Although you don't eat the leaf, it adds a lovely tannic smokiness to the fish.

PEPES IKAN

SERVES 4

4 generous pieces of banana leaf
800g white fish fillet, cut into 4 even-sized pieces
1 lime, quartered, to serve

for the spice paste
3 garlic cloves, peeled
1 banana shallot, roughly chopped
2cm piece fresh root ginger, roughly chopped
1 stalk lemongrass, outer leaves discarded, inner roughly chopped
25g candlenuts (about 8), or macadamia nuts
1 teaspoon tamarind concentrate, or 1 tablespoon tamarind pulp
1 teaspoon dried chilli flakes
½ teaspoon ground turmeric
¼ teaspoon shrimp paste
1 large red tomato, roughly chopped
salt and freshly ground black pepper

you will need
cocktail sticks to secure the banana leaves

Place the garlic, shallot, ginger, lemongrass, candlenuts, tamarind, chilli, turmeric, shrimp paste and tomato in a food processor. With the motor running, add just enough water, about 1–2 tablespoons, to make a smooth, thick paste. Season to taste. Alternatively, place all the ingredients in a deep jug and pulse with a stick blender until smooth.

Lay out the banana leaves and put a piece of fish in the middle of each. Divide the spice paste evenly between the fish, spreading it out all over. Fold up the ends of the banana leaf and roll up tightly so the fish is completely covered. Pin each end securely with a cocktail stick to stop it from opening up. Set aside on the worktop for 20–30 minutes to marinate.

While the fish is marinating, fire up the barbecue until hot, or preheat a large griddle pan. Cook the fish parcels for about 4 minutes on each side, until the banana leaf is nicely charred on the outside. Carefully unwrap one parcel to check the fish is cooked through – it will be opaque and flake easily when teased with a fork.

Serve the parcels with a wedge of lime to squeeze over once unwrapped.

Ayam goreng take-out shops and roadside stalls are found all over Indonesia – they are basically fried chicken joints, and who doesn't love a bit of crisply fried chicken? The pieces of meat are marinated for several hours then simmered until cooked through before frying. This is great as it eases the 'is it cooked properly?' pressures we often associate with chicken. *Sambal bajak* is a fiery roast chilli paste. If you prefer less heat I suggest serving the chicken with the *sambal kecap* recipe on page 262.

Note: you will need to begin this recipe several hours before you want to eat, or ideally the day before, to allow the chicken to marinate.

AYAM GORENG WITH SAMBAL BAJAK

SERVES 4–6, DEPENDING ON GREED OR HUNGER!

1 large chicken (about 2.5kg), or a selection of bone-in chicken pieces
2 bay leaves
500g banana shallots, sliced into 5mm rings

for the spice paste
2 tablespoons coriander seeds
8 garlic cloves, roughly chopped
3 banana shallots, roughly chopped
3 stalks of lemongrass, outer leaves discarded, inner roughly chopped
75g fresh root ginger, roughly chopped
50g candlenuts or macadamia nuts
50g fresh turmeric root, roughly chopped
salt and freshly ground black pepper

for the sambal bajak
100g red bird's-eye chillies, stalks removed (remove the seeds for less heat)
100g shallots, thickly sliced
100g cherry tomatoes
6 fat garlic cloves, roughly chopped
6 candlenuts or macadamia nuts
6 kaffir lime leaves, thinly sliced
1 tablespoon shrimp paste
1 tablespoon soft brown sugar
1 teaspoon salt
1 tablespoon vegetable oil

For the spice paste, place the coriander seeds in a small frying pan and toast over a medium heat for a minute or two until you can smell their aroma wafting up from the pan. Tip into a spice mill or pestle and mortar and grind coarsely. Add to a food processor, along with the garlic, shallots, lemongrass, ginger, candlenuts and turmeric. Season generously. Whizz to a paste, adding just enough cold water to help it along – a couple of tablespoons should do it.

Joint the chicken into 10 pieces: 2 drumsticks, 2 thighs, each breast chopped into 2, plus 2 wings. A combination of small, sharp knife and scissors is the easiest way to do this, following the joints and bones as a guide. Don't worry if it looks a little rough and ready. Add the pieces to a large shallow dish in a single layer and dollop the spice paste on top, rubbing it all over. Cover and marinate in the fridge for a few hours, or ideally overnight.

Transfer the chicken, along with any excess marinade, into a large stockpot. Add the bay leaves and just enough cold water to cover the chicken and set over a high heat to bring to the boil. Reduce the heat to a steady simmer, cover with a loose-fitting lid and cook for 30 minutes. Use a slotted spoon to transfer the chicken to a large plate. Discard the poaching liquor, or even better, strain it and use it as the stock base of an Asian soup. It will freeze well if you want to save it.

To make the *sambal bajak*, put all the ingredients except the oil into a food processor and pulse to a thick paste. Add the oil to a frying pan and set over a medium-high heat. Once hot, scrape in the paste and stir fry for about 8–10 minutes until the sauce turns a shade darker and is rich and thick. Reduce the heat a little if it begins to stick. The *sambal bajak* will keep well in the fridge for up to 3 weeks, covered with a layer of cling film pressed to the surface.

While the chicken is poaching, heat the oil in a deep fat fryer to 180°C/350°F. When the oil is hot, add the shallot rings and allow to fry for a few minutes until golden and crisp. Shake any excess oil back into the fryer and tip on to kitchen paper to drain. Set aside.

Deep fry the poached chicken in batches of 3 or 4 pieces for about 5 minutes each until they are a deep golden brown.

Serve the chicken sprinkled with the crisp shallots, with the *sambal bajak* on the side.

School prawns are one of my favourite fried treats to cook throughout the summer here in Australia. A smaller, sweeter and more affordable version of their big brother, the green king prawn, they're the perfect moreish bar snack. And the best bit is that you get to eat the whole thing, head and all! It can be tricky to get hold of school prawns, so king prawns can be substituted, but should be barbecued rather than deep fried – I've given both recipes below.

FRIED SCHOOL PRAWNS WITH CITRUS SALT AND SRIRACHA MAYO

 Andy Allen
MasterChef Australia, 2012 Champion

SERVES 4, AS A SNACK

2 litres groundnut oil, for frying
350g raw school prawns or king
    prawns (shell on)
finely sliced red and green
    chillies, to garnish
lime wedges, to serve (optional)

for the citrus salt
3 tablespoons sea salt flakes
grated zest of 2 small limes

for the Sriracha mayonnaise
4 tablespoons kewpie
    mayonnaise (or any
    homemade mayonnaise)
2 tablespoons Sriracha sauce
juice of 1 lime
1 teaspoon sea salt flakes

for the seasoned flour (school prawns only)
150g rice flour
2 teaspoons fine salt flakes
1 tablespoon chilli powder
½ tablespoon garlic powder
1 teaspoon mustard powder
1 teaspoon white pepper

To make the citrus salt, combine the sea salt flakes and lime zest in a small bowl and set aside.

For the Sriracha mayonnaise, place the kewpie mayonnaise and Sriracha sauce in a bowl, then add the lime juice and salt and mix all the ingredients together. Taste, and if you're happy, bang it in your serving bowl and set aside.

If using school prawns, make the seasoned flour. Place all the ingredients in a large bowl. Mix well, then add the school prawns and give them a good toss, making sure they're all covered in the flour. In a large pan, heat the oil to 200°C/390°F. Before frying, shake off any excess flour from the school prawns. This will make sure the oil stays nice and hot, which will give you a crisper, tastier prawn. Once the oil is hot, submerge the prawns in the oil and fry for a minute. Remove the prawns from the fryer, transfer to kitchen paper and season with the citrus salt while the prawns are still hot.

If using king prawns, fire up a barbecue until medium-hot and cook the prawns for 2 minutes each side until pink. Season with the citrus salt while the prawns are still hot.

To serve, make a nice mound of the prawns on your serving plate along with a generous ramekin of the Sriracha mayo and some extra citrus salt; garnish with some finely sliced red and green chillies and lime wedges.

Chiko rolls are the Australian equivalent of a spring roll. The traditional fare of sporting matches in their native Oz, these are not dainty little things but rather a big, stuffed-to-the-gunnels snack that will fill you up nicely. The peppery filling reminds me a little of a proper Cornish pasty, with the added texture of chewy pearl barley.

CHIKO ROLLS

MAKES 16 LARGE ROLLS

100g pearl barley
2 tablespoons olive oil
1 onion, finely chopped
1 stick celery, finely chopped
1 carrot, finely diced
200g white cabbage, finely
  shredded
350g cooked roast lamb or beef,
  finely chopped
1 beef stock cube
salt and freshly ground black
  pepper
tomato ketchup and/or chilli
  sauce, to serve

for the egg roll wrappers
500g plain flour
1 large egg
175ml ice-cold water
a pinch of salt
cornflour, for rolling

Soak the pearl barley in cold water for an hour, then drain well and place in a saucepan. Cover well with boiling water and simmer for about 15–20 minutes, until tender. Drain and set aside.

Meanwhile, place the olive oil in a large frying pan and set over a medium-low heat. Add the onion, celery and carrot and fry gently for 10 minutes until starting to soften, then add the cabbage and season generously with salt and pepper, and fry for a further 10 minutes. Stir through the chopped meat and pearl barley, crumble in the stock cube and pour in 125ml water, cooking for a further 10 minutes until the liquid has virtually evaporated. Turn off the heat and leave to cool.

To make the wrappers, add the flour, egg, water and salt to a food mixer fitted with a dough hook. Knead for about 5 minutes until you have a smooth, stretchy dough, You can also make this dough by hand by mixing everything together in a bowl, then tipping on to a lightly oiled worktop and kneading until smooth; it will take about 10 minutes by hand. Chop the dough into 16 even-sized pieces and roll each into a ball. Set on a baking tray, cover with a clean tea towel and leave to rest for 30 minutes.

When you are ready to assemble the chiko rolls, lightly dust the worktop with cornflour. Take a piece of dough and roll it out to a 2mm-thin square about 16 x 16cm. Spoon 3 tablespoons of filling along the bottom edge, leaving a generous 4cm margin at either side and at the base. Lift up the left and right edges and lay them over the filling, keeping them parallel. Then roll up tightly so the filling is covered by a couple of layers of wrapper. Brush the back edge with a little water before sealing up all the way. Rest on a baking tray that's lightly dusted with a little cornflour and repeat with the remaining dough and filling.

Once they are all rolled, heat the oil in a deep fat fryer to 180°C/350°F. Fry the chiko rolls in batches of 3 for about 5 minutes until deep golden brown. Serve immediately, when they will be crispest, or allow them to cool a little, when the pastry will become lovely and chewy. Serve with bowls of ketchup and/or chilli sauce to dunk them in as you eat.

For me, food is all about an experience and creating memories that develop into triggers of nostalgia. A steak and onion pie is exactly this. As a young chap I remember sitting on the damp wooden seats at Waverly Park, waiting for my beloved Essendon Bombers to go into an AFL battle. Dad would be attempting to shield me from the raindrops that would inevitably penetrate my thick bomber jacket, and I would continue to take another careless bite into the pool of volcanic beef and onion stew that was encased in a bowl of sweet buttery pastry, knowing that my tongue would be scorched but my stomach would receive a warm dose of happiness. Here, I've jazzed up the humble steak and onion pie to dazzle your diners, but the memory behind it is the most important part.

STEAK AND ONION PIE, ONLY BETTER

Brent Owens
MasterChef Australia, 2014 Champion

SERVES 4

2 tablespoons olive oil
2 x 600g beef cheeks, sinew trimmed
1 large onion, cut into wedges
2 garlic cloves, crushed
125ml red wine
1 litre beef stock
2 sprigs rosemary
1 x 320g pack (1 sheet) shop-bought puff pastry
1 small knob of butter
salt and freshly ground black pepper
1 stick celery, finely diced, to garnish
celery leaves, to garnish
nasturtium leaves, to garnish

for the sweet tomato relish
250g ripe tomatoes
½ red onion, finely diced
1 teaspoon olive oil
1 garlic clove, finely diced
¼ teaspoon dried chilli flakes
½ teaspoon tomato paste or purée
1 tablespoon brown sugar
1 tablespoon red wine vinegar

for the smoky soured onions
1 teaspoon olive oil
4 shallots, cut in half lengthways
125ml apple cider vinegar
1 tablespoon caster sugar

For the sweet tomato relish, cut a shallow cross in the bottom of each tomato using a small knife. Place the tomatoes in a large bowl, cover with boiling water and leave for 30 seconds, then immediately transfer the tomatoes into a bowl of iced water. Peel the tomatoes and set aside. Cut the cooled tomatoes into quarters, remove and discard the inner membranes and seeds, and chop the flesh into small chunks.

While the tomatoes are cooling, place a medium-sized saucepan over a medium heat. Add the onion and olive oil and cook for 4–6 minutes until soft but not coloured. Add the garlic and chilli flakes and cook for a further minute. Add the tomato paste or purée and stir for 2 minutes, then add the sugar and vinegar. Add the tomatoes to the saucepan and give the mixture a good stir. Bring to the boil then reduce the heat to medium-low. Cook for 8–10 minutes, stirring occasionally, until the mixture is thick and gloopy. Season with salt and pepper and set aside to cool slightly.

Once cooled, blitz the mixture with a stick blender or transfer into a liquidizer and pulse to form a smooth paste. Remove and set aside until ready to serve.

To make the smoky soured onions, put the olive oil in a small frying pan over a medium-high heat and season the oil with salt. Place the onions, cut side down, in an even layer around the frying pan. Cook for 4–6 minutes, or until lightly charred, then reduce the heat to low and add the vinegar and sugar. Cover and cook over a low heat for a further 5 minutes, then turn off the heat and leave the onions to cool in the liquid. Set aside until ready to serve.

Preheat the oven to 190°C/170°C Fan/Gas Mark 5. Heat the olive oil in a deep flameproof casserole dish over a high heat. Season the beef cheeks with salt and pepper, add them to the pan and cook until golden on both sides, about 2–4 minutes. Remove the meat from the pan and transfer to a plate. Reduce the heat to medium, add the onion and cook for 4–5 minutes. Add the garlic and cook for a further minute. Increase the heat to high and add the red wine. Cook to reduce for 2 minutes then return the beef to the pan and add the beef stock and rosemary. Bring to the boil, cover and transfer to the oven. Cook for 2½–4 hours, or until the cheeks are able to be pulled apart with a fork, but still hold their shape. Once the cheeks are cooked, remove from the liquid and set aside to cool, reserving the cooking liquid.

While the cheeks are cooling, increase the oven heat to 200°C/180°C Fan/Gas Mark 6. Line a large baking tray with baking parchment. Cut the puff pastry into 4 small discs, around 10cm in diameter, and place them on the baking tray. Place another sheet of baking parchment over the top and weigh it down with another baking tray of a similar size. Bake in the oven for 10–12 minutes, until the pastry is crisp and golden. Remove from the oven and set aside.

Meanwhile, place the cooking liquid in the casserole dish on to the hob over a high heat. Stir in the butter, season with salt and pepper and strain through a fine sieve. Cut the cooled cheeks into 4 large cubes and dip them into the sauce until well coated.

To assemble, place the beef cheeks on to individual plates. Spoon over a few tablespoons of the remaining sauce. Add small blobs of the tomato relish then place the onions on top. Place a pastry disc over the top of the beef and garnish with diced celery and the celery and nasturtium leaves.

INDEX

ACKNOWLEDGEMENTS AND CREDITS

Genevieve Taylor would like to thank....

I have had such fun writing this MasterChef Street Food book – what a joy is has been to research, cook and eat my way around the world. The writing and testing of recipes are just one process of creating a great cook book, and I'd like to thank the whole team for their individual parts that make up the whole gorgeous thing you have in front of you. Everybody at Shine has been brilliant, and thanks are due to the fabulous MasterChef contributors from around the globe who have added much expertise and local knowledge in their recipes.

Absolute Press has, yet again, done me proud. Emily North (Project Editor) Kim Musgrove (Designer) and Jon Croft (Publisher and general grand fromage) – thanks to you all. Big thanks to Rachel Malig for her excellent nips and tucks to my words, and to my fabulous agent, Kate Hordern for steering my path calmly and sensibly.

It has been such an honour to work once again with David Loftus, who's photos are indeed legendary, but also because of the quiet, calm and happy way he goes about capturing beauty. Thanks so much David. And also huge thanks to the extremely creative and very lovely Ange Morris who's prop styling enhances my food no end. I was ably assisted on the photoshoots by some really great food stylists – Danielle Combes, Laura Field, Jennifer Henry, Laura Rowe, Helen Upshall – it was so great to have all your steady hands in the kitchen!

Last but clearly not least – what is a cookbook without a legion of willing family and friends to eat the spoils of my cooking? It's been so good to share the bounty with you all. Big love.

Shine would like to thank...

First and foremost, the thirteen brilliant MasterChef champions who contributed recipes to this collection: Andy Allen, Tim Anderson, Dhruv Baker, Marc Boissieux, Ping Coombes, Christine Ha, Anders Halskov-Jensen, Adam Liaw, Luca Manfè, Brent Owens, Claudia Sandoval, Woo Wai Leong and Simon Wood. Shine would also like to thank Claire Burton.

Publisher Jon Croft
Commissioning Editor Meg Avent
Project Editor Emily North
Art Director and Designer Kim Musgrove
Design Consultant Claire Burton
Photographer David Loftus
Prop stylist Ange Morris
Food Stylist Genevieve Taylor
Assistant food stylists Danielle Combes, Laura Field, Jennifer Henry, Laura Rowe, Helen Upshall
Editor Rachel Malig
Proofreader Eleanor Van Zandt
Indexer Zoe Ross

CONVERSION TABLES

Weights

Metric	Imperial
15g	½oz
20g	¾oz
30g	1oz
55g	2oz
85g	3oz
110g	4oz / ¼lb
140g	5oz
170g	6oz
200g	7oz
225g	8oz / ½lb
255g	9oz
285g	10oz
310g	11oz
340g	12oz / ¾lb
370g	13oz
400g	14oz
425g	15oz
450g	16oz / 1lb
1kg	2lb 4oz
1.5kg	3lb 5oz

Liquids

Metric	Imperial
5ml	1 teaspoon
15ml	1 tablespoon or ½fl oz
30ml	2 tablespoons or 1fl oz
150ml	¼ pint or 5fl oz
290ml	½ pint or 10fl oz
425ml	¾ pint or 16fl oz
570ml	1 pint or 20fl oz
1 litre	1¾ pints
1.2 litres	2 pints

Length

Metric	Imperial
5mm	¼in
1cm	½in
2cm	¾in
2.5cm	1in
5cm	2in
10cm	4in
15cm	6in
20cm	8in
30cm	12in

Useful conversions

1 tablespoon = 3 teaspoons

1 level tablespoon = approx. 15g or ½oz

1 heaped tablespoon = approx. 30g or 1oz

1 egg = 55ml / 55g / 1fl oz